KU-186-596

The Changing Face of Education 14 to 16: Curriculum and Assessment

Edited by
Sally Brown and Pamela Munn

With contributions from
Sally Brown
Bob Currie
Eric Drever
Margaret Eleftheriou
Thomas Johnson
Donald McIntyre
Peter Martin
Pamela Munn
Mary Simpson
Douglas Weir

NFER-NELSON

Published by the NFER-NELSON Publishing Company Ltd.,
Darville House, 2 Oxford Road East,
Windsor, Berkshire SL4 1DF

and in the United States of America by

NFER-NELSON, 242 Cherry Street, Philadelphia, PA 19106–1906.
Tel: (215) 238 0939. Telex: 244489

First Published 1985
© 1985, Sally Brown and Pamela Munn
© for individual chapters remains with the authors
Library of Congress Cataloging in Publication data

All rights reserved, including translation. No part
of this publication may be reproduced or transmitted
in any form or by any means, electronic or mechanical,
including photocopying, recording or duplication in
any information storage and retrieval system, without
permission in writing from the publishers.

Printed by Billing and Sons Ltd, Worcester

ISBN 0 7005 1017 6
Code 8205 02 1

For Bill Nicol
who did so much
to encourage
educational research
in Scotland

Contents

Preface

Educational commentators have been prone to report that Scotland was the first part of the United Kingdom to respond to the call for action which came from the 'Great Debate' about education in the late seventies. This is not the place to argue about whether the new developments in Scotland were in fact a result of the initiation of that debate rather than part of a much longer-term evolution in the Scottish system of education. What is important is that they heralded a decade in which not only educators but also the public at large would be expected to scrutinize and reassess what had previously been seen as fundamental tenets of education.

The chairmen of two committees, which were set up by the Secretary of State for Scotland and reported in 1977, had their names immortalized in the 'Munn and Dunning Developments'. These developments in the curriculum and assessment for 14- to 16-year-olds set the scene for some profound changes in the way we think about education in Scotland. That changed thinking has produced new curricula, new systems of assessment and a new form of national certification. These have been accompanied by a wealth of official documents from the Scottish Education Department and the Scottish Examination Board and publications about specialist aspects of the developments from professional researchers. What have been less in evidence, and this is probably because everyone has been so busy getting on with the development work, are publications which take a broader and more reflective view of the programme as a whole.

This book has attempted to take such a view of particular features of the programme. It is concerned with the description and analysis of changes which have been attempted in assessment and the curriculum, including criterion-referenced assessment, diagnostic assessment, certification for all secondary school pupils, school validated components for certification, mastery learning, process learning, new teaching methods and school-based curriculum development. It concentrates on those aspects of the developments which have implications for the professional lives of teachers and it explores how the research which has been a part of the development programme supports and informs educational policy and practice.

The distinctive features of the developments on which the book is focused are by no means solely the concern of Scottish educators or relevant only to the 14 to 16 age group. Almost all of the innovations which are described have implications for the professional practice of teachers. We hope that accounts of what the innovations mean for those who have had to put them into practice will be of interest and practical benefit to educators throughout the United Kingdom and elsewhere. It is for the wide audience of teachers, student teachers, teacher-educators, curriculum developers, examination board officers, advisers, Her Majesty's Inspectors and researchers with interests and involvement in secondary education that this book is written.

All the contributors to the book have been intimately involved in the research or the developments of the Munn and Dunning programme. They include teachers, researchers, lecturers (university and college of education) and the director of a vocational preparation unit. While we hope that this will give the book a broad perspective on the development programme, we are by no means claiming to offer a comprehensive picture of this ambitious and important national enterprise. Our intention is to complement the views expressed in extant 'official' publications and to contribute in a constructive way to the continuing debate on education.

Several chapters in this book are based on work which has been carried out in circumstances where the authors were in receipt of funding from the Scottish Education Department. That support is gratefully acknowledged and provides an indication of the importance which that Department has placed on a thorough exploration of the changes to be made in education 14 to 16. Any views expressed or conclusions drawn in the book, however, are those of the authors and are not necessarily shared by the Scottish Education Department.

Finally, we would like to express our thanks to Edna Kentley and Jennifer McDonald; without their efforts and skill in typing the manuscript, this book could not have been produced.

May 1985

NFER-NELSON

ed. S Brown & P. Munn

1985

CHAPTER 1
The Changing Face of Education
14 to 16 : Curriculum & Assessment

Pamela Munn and Sally Brown

The Emergence of the Development Programme

'Munn and Dunning' is now an established phrase in Scottish education. It has proved versatile, being used sometimes as a noun, as in 'We're doing Munn and Dunning' and sometimes as an adjective, as in 'These are our Munn and Dunning modules'. Use of the phrase in conversation is a risky business, however, as reactions are unpredictable. They can include bewilderment, fury, or enthusiasm. The phrase has almost the same characteristics, versatility and unpredictability as the educational programme it is used to describe. This programme, first begun in 1979, claimed origins in two reports published by the Scottish Education Department (SED) in 1977 on the curriculum and assessment of 14- to 16-year-olds in Scottish secondary schools. The reports were the products of two committees set up to investigate these matters. Their chairmen, Dr Munn and Mr Dunning, have given their names to these reports and are destined to be forever linked in public consciousness as one of the great 'double acts' in Scottish education.

The background to the establishment of the committees was one of unease about curriculum provision and assessment policy in Scottish secondary schools. Following the raising of the school leaving age and the widespread establishment of comprehensive schools, there was concern about the balance, nature and quality of the curriculum being offered to 14- to 16-year-olds. There was also concern about the appropriacy of the 'O' grade as the target examination for increasing numbers of 16-year-olds.

Originally set up to service a minority of pupils, by 1976 it was clear that the examination was being attempted by pupils for whom it had never been intended (SED, 1977b). The inflexibility of the 'O' grade had prompted some teachers to turn to other forms of assessment and certification for their pupils, such as the Certificate of Secondary Education (CSE). The CSE was offered by examination boards in England and Wales and through its Mode III presentation gave teachers a greater role in syllabus design and assessment than the 'O' grade. Although each committee had a distinct and separate remit, the Munn Committee being concerned with the curriculum and the Dunning Committee with assessment, they kept in touch with each other, and publicly reported simultaneously.

The Munn Report (SED, 1977a, pp.21–22) identified four main sets of aims for secondary schools as a means of determining the general scope of the curriculum. The committee was concerned that the curriculum should generate in pupils: (i) 'knowledge and understanding, both of the self and of the social and physical environment', (ii) skills including the cognitive, interpersonal and psychomotor, (iii) affective development, and (iv) a capability 'to perform the various roles which life in their society entails'. In addition, the committee used 'modes of activity' or 'ways of knowing' as an analytical tool for constructing the curriculum. From these starting points, a 'compulsory core' curriculum of seven areas of study was constructed. These areas were English, Mathematical Skills, Physical Education, Religious/Moral Education, Science, Social Studies and Creative Arts. Every pupil would be exposed to these areas of study. Beyond this, there were to be elective areas from which pupils could choose to study, say, a language other than English, and practical or vocational subjects such as business studies or home economics. The committee endorsed the single subject as the basic unit of study in both the 'core' and 'elective' areas, although it did advocate experimentation with multi-disciplinary courses.

The Dunning Report (SED, 1977b) saw assessment as integral to teaching and learning rather than as a separate 'testing' exercise. It advocated that all pupils completing S4 should be awarded a certificate of secondary education. It proposed that there should be three levels of award, Foundation, General and Credit, to cater for pupils' abilities, with five sub-grades across the three levels. In determining pupils' grades, the report called for a greater role for teachers and recommended that they be positively involved in syllabus design and assessment procedures. National certificates were to be based partly on external and partly on school assessment. The report also advocated that studies should be undertaken 'to determine the relevance and applicability of criterion-referenced tests to different subjects'.

Both reports produced a considerable reaction in Scotland, favourable and unfavourable. The suggestions they made for educational change were varied in the sense that some were put forward with conviction and others with circumspection. Many of the proposals reflected ambitious goals, but some people felt that few were clearly articulated and that the descriptions offered displayed a variety of inconsistencies (e.g. Kirk, 1982 and McIntyre, 1978). It was not until 1979 that plans to go ahead with a series of feasibility studies on 'Munn and Dunning' were announced. The overall purpose of these feasibility studies was to advise the Secretary of State for Scotland on the wider scale implementation of changes in curriculum and assessment. The decision was made to concentrate initially on developments at Foundation level and to focus on English, mathematics and science with three multi-disciplinary courses following a year later. In particular, these studies were concerned with testing the feasibility of extending to teachers more responsibilities following the Munn and Dunning Reports' recommendations 'that internal syllabus design and internal assessment should permit flexibility of approach, while maintaining national standards of attainment by use of an external syllabus component and an element of external assessment' (SED, 1980, p.8).

The experiences of the feasibility studies, in which teachers and pilot schools were involved on a substantial scale in curriculum and assessment developments, led to a decision in 1982 by the Secretary of State to press ahead with change. Developments in all subjects are now either in full swing or about to begin. Indeed, we are now witnessing an unprecedented national programme of development in the curriculum and assessment of 14- to 16-year-olds in Scottish schools. It is interesting, however, that the development model adopted for the major part of the programme post-1982 (SED, 1982) is not that of the earlier feasibility studies. It relies instead on centrally constituted Joint Working Parties (JWPs) of the Consultative Committee on the Curriculum (CCC) and the Scottish Examination Board (SEB), which have remits in each subject area to formulate national guidelines for syllabus and assessment and recommend the arrangements for certification. The earlier emphasis on the direct involvement of pilot schools and teachers in helping to formulate and pilot curriculum and assessment plans has been substantially reduced.

Distinctive Features of the Programme

This book neither attempts to describe all the developments nor offers a critique of the programme as a whole. Our approach has been to concentrate on what seem to us to be the distinctive features of the programme. We use 'distinctive' in the sense of implying some kind of change in the realities of schooling for both teachers and pupils. It is our intention that the book as a whole should offer insights into the emergence, development, dissemination and implications for implementation of the various ideas and innovations which distinguish the programme. We are not directly concerned with those aspects of the programme which have evolved in a way which suggests little or no change for pupils and teachers, although reference is made to such aspects in some of the chapters.

We have identified five features which we regard as distinctive:

(i) The programme incorporated an experiment which explored a more school-based procedure for development based on extended dialogue and collaboration with teachers on curriculum, assessment and teaching approaches. This experiment and the questions it raised about the locus of control for decision making and the pace of the development have had substantial implications for the courses and assessment schemes which have been generated.

(ii) Considerable emphasis has been put on a new conception of assessment as an integral part of the curriculum and a support for learning rather than as a separate 'testing' exercise. This has signalled a move away from the view that assessment is a highly technical activity which is fully understood only by psychometricians and not by teachers. It implies, however, that teachers should be aiming to introduce such things as systematic diagnostic assessment in the classroom. Existing assessment procedures, familiar teaching strategies and the time available will clearly be stretched to achieve such aims. The new conception of assessment then clearly implies some change in classroom practice at a number of levels.

(iii) The proposed innovation in certification offers certificates for all and not, as previously, for just the more able pupils. It has stimulated explorations of the possibilities of using criterion-referencing or Grade Related Criteria to provide descriptive accounts of what has been attained. Furthermore, it has given teachers some responsibility for the assessment of their pupils for national certificate awards. Such proposals faced substantial questions about the assessment load on teachers, problems of comparability across schools, complexity of certificate reports (which have traditionally been administratively simple) and dangers of the lowest level of award ('Foundation') being equated with 'Fail'.

(iv) The variety of new ways of defining the knowledge to be acquired by pupils (e.g. a multi-disciplinary course in Social and Vocational Skills or Listening Skills in English) and the role of the teacher in facilitating this acquisition (e.g. the non-directive management of pupils' discussions) provided another innovative facet of the developments. Given the traditional notion of the teacher as the fountain of knowledge for pupils, these kinds of innovations would clearly present some difficulties.

(v) Within the main developments was included a substantial research programme designed to support and inform policy and practice. But can research be set up to fulfil such functions? How do teachers and others perceive the role and value of such research?

The contributions from the different chapters of this book reflect a variety of perspectives on these distinctive features since their authors include teachers, college of education lecturers, lecturers in university education departments and researchers in education. Some contributions concern predominantly one distinctive feature, others two or more in a variety of combinations. What all the contributions have in common, however, is a concern for the impact of the developments upon the classroom. For this reason, we hope the book as a whole will be of interest not only to those most immediately affected by 'Munn and Dunning' – teachers, parents and pupils in Scotland – but to a wider audience contemplating changes in curriculum and assessment, or more generally interested in the attempts to apply ideas on such diverse matters as, say, criterion-referencing, school-based curriculum development and process learning.

The Contributions

We have tried to group the chapters in terms of their predominant concern with changes in the curriculum, teaching methods or assessment. Within this arrangement the contributions are sequenced so that the reader is taken progressively from accounts of individual or school experience of change to those with a wider focus.

Margaret Eleftheriou's chapter concerns the changes which have taken place in the English curriculum. From the perspective of Head of English in a comprehensive school, she describes her own department's radical conception of 'Foundation' as a stage through which all pupils studying English would pass and the consequent rethinking of the whole English curriculum with 'new ideas springing up everywhere'. These ideas spilled over into assessment and she describes attempts to devise assessments which would assess the four modes of English – reading, writing, speaking and listening – in a valid and reliable way. The chapter, however, also provides a graphic description of the development process itself, the leisurely pace and experimental approach encouraging diverse approaches to English at the early developmental phase being in stark contrast to later phases emphasizing speed and progress. The evolution of national Grade Related Criteria is described in this context.

The development process is also a feature of Douglas Weir's and Bob Currie's chapter on Social and Vocational Skills. They give us a view, from the stance of researchers/developers, not only of relationships between the schools and the centre, but also of the role of a collaborative action research project in the curriculum development process. Social and Vocational Skills was a radical curriculum innovation on a number of levels. First, it was a course adopting a multi-disciplinary approach and not rooted exclusively in any single subject traditionally to be found in Scottish secondary schools. Secondly, it defined itself as new and distinctive in terms of the processes incorporated in the course, not in syllabus content. Thirdly, it implicitly challenged traditional perceptions of the teacher as expert purveyor of specialized knowledge to 'lay' pupils. This chapter offers a description of both the evolution of the course and its accommodation within a national framework of assessment and syllabus validation.

Pamela Munn takes a reseacher's look at all three multi-disciplinary courses being piloted as part of a development programme which had endorsed the single subject as the basic unit of study. She concentrates on the kinds of collaboration teachers saw the courses as requiring and on the factors affecting that collaboration. The courses are viewed as presenting challenges to school organization and management and more fundamentally to notions of teacher professionalism, constructed on the possession of subject specialist knowledge and teaching skills. She suggests a number of dimensions of collaboration and invites teachers interested in multi-disciplinary developments to use these dimensions as a checklist for the kinds of collaboration most appropriate for them. Finally, a range of incentives towards collaboration are considered and the different reactions of teachers to school-based development as an incentive are reported.

Many of the curriculum changes encouraged by the development programme have been accompanied by calls for experiments in innovative teaching methods. Tom Johnson, a principal teacher of modern studies in a comprehensive school, argues indeed that while the programme has advocated new teaching methods, there has been a failure to make clear what these mean for classroom life. Teachers, he says, are being asked to promote and assess programmes in these new methods for which they have little or no training. This chapter describes his experience both of a training programme in discussion and his experience of implementing discussion programmes in the classroom. The individual skills involved in small group discussion are illustrated and his collaboration with colleagues and pupils in articulating these skills and in testing hypotheses about them are described. He is, like Douglas Weir, convinced of the worthwhileness of a 'process approach' to learning, but is aware of the constraints of implementing such an approach in his own school far less on a national basis.

From the stance of a lecturer in a university department of education with a strong commitment to research, Eric Drever's chapter also concerns innovative teaching approaches. His are associated with a curriculum embodying 'mastery learning' principles. He discusses some implications of a mastery learning approach, paying particular attention to Bloom's (1976) central idea that we need to abandon the traditional explanations of success and failure in school learning as due to differences in pupils' general ability. One school's attempts to implement mastery learning across the curriculum are described. Examples of work done on the school report, on informal diagnostic assessment and on remedial education are used to show that when teachers do abandon the notion of general ability as an explanation of pupils' failure to learn, and base even a limited area of practice on mastery learning, then they report the benefits that Bloom claims of improved pupil performance and motivation. Eric Drever also argues, however, that there are important practical and ideological obstacles to introducing the new approach, of which Bloom himself has little to say. Present styles of school decision making and in-service training do not seem to be well suited to cope with these obstacles. A possible conclusion is that Bloom's ideas need to be incorporated into the processes of innovation, and applied not only to pupils' but to teachers' learning.

The challenge to the value and validity of general ability as an explanation of pupils' failure to learn is introduced by Eric Drever, and developed by Mary Simpson, a researcher with special interest in assessment. She argues that pupils are active, continuous creators of their own understanding rather than passive, impotent accumulators of given knowledge. Evidence is offered, from research on learning difficulties in science, that such difficulties can arise from traditional teaching methods. A case is presented for methods which (i) ensure that pupils possess the necessary background knowledge before they are required to learn new material and (ii) are sensitive to the possiblity of pupils developing idiosyncratic and incorrect understanding of the information they have acquired from school and other experiences. Diagnostic assessment requires attention to be paid to wrong answers and to the ways in which the wrong ideas underlying these answers have developed. Mary Simpson speculates that fundamental change in assessment policy and practice will not take place until the myth of general ability is exploded and that this will not happen by 'big bang' curriculum development but through the steady stream of local innovation by teachers.

Although Peter Martin, a college of education lecturer, is also sceptical about the extent of real change in assessment policy, he argues that a national model of criterion-referenced certification is more likely to bring about such change than school-based initiatives. His views, then, are in direct contrast to those of Mary Simpson and Eric Drever. He describes such a model which incorporates detailed criterion-referenced assessment for both reporting and diagnostic purposes and aggregation of pupil attainments using explicit rules. In the short term, such a model would permit teachers to do diagnostic testing, but still meet the needs of the Scottish Examination Board for teachers' (i) assessments of pupils for certification at Foundation level, and (ii) estimates of pupils' grades and evidence for comparison with external grades for certification at General and Credit levels. He asserts that if criterion-referenced certification can be established, then a genuinely new and better era will be starting. The challenge he makes to the teaching profession is to decide just how much it wants such radical changes.

The difficulties of promoting change in teachers' classroom practice is the focus of the chapter by Donald McIntyre (a reader in a university department of education). He puts forward the case for a school-based approach to curriculum development and asks how genuinely school based the government's programme has been. He describes the main characteristics of educational planning in Scotland in the past, and sees these characteristics as still dominant despite early attempts to involve a wide range of teachers in decision making. His analysis of the current development context leads him to conclude that changes in the realities of classroom life for most pupils and teachers will be superficial.

Sally Brown, as a university senior research fellow, takes an overview of the role of research in the development programme. She describes the different kinds of research which were sponsored and their different purposes, including the tensions between research and development. The role of research in the development programme is analysed and consideration is given to the practical lessons to be learned by (i) researchers who wish their work to have an impact on practitioners and policymakers, and (ii) those who may have responsibilities in the future for decisions on research as a part of national developments.

A number of themes runs through the various contributions, although individual authors present different perspectives on these themes. A dominant theme is the tension between a programme of national proportions on the one hand and local school or teacher initiatives on the other. This is reflected not only in curriculum development where boundaries between national syllabus guidelines and teachers' own initiatives varied across courses, but also in assessment. Here competing pressures of implementing a new national system of assessment which would have public confidence and of teachers' own initiatives and experiments are evident. The chapters by Margaret Eleftheriou, Douglas Weir, Peter Martin and Donald McIntyre demonstrate these competing pressures in curriculum and assessment.

A second theme is that of constraints both in terms of school organization and management and in terms of teacher ideologies of implementing some of the innovations in the development programme. Schools organized in terms of discrete subject departments pose problems for multi-disciplinary courses, for instance. Ideologies of teacher professionalism, and of pupils' general ability as a convincing explanation of failure to learn can inhibit innovations in curriculum and assessment. Chapters by Pamela Munn, Eric Drever and Mary Simpson consider these kinds of constraints on innovation. Courses which challenge the dominance of subject specific expertise and call for innovative methods of teaching and assessment are problematic indeed.

Lastly, the role of research in the development process is a major theme. Sally Brown's chapter deals with this most explicitly and comprehensively, but it is significant that almost all of the contributions here relate directly or indirectly to research as part of the programme. This applies not only to chapters written by professional researchers but also to those written by teachers. Tom Johnson refers to the central importance of work done on discussion skills in Moray House College of Education in his chapter and Margaret Eleftheriou talks about her deep involvement with the trials for the research on reading.

We hope that there will be other books written about this major educational development with perspectives different from ours. The development programme has been an enormous undertaking and there are many ways in which Scottish education will never be the same again. Taken together, we believe the contributions to this book provide an analysis of some aspects of the developments, but they identify only a few of the features of the 'Munn and Dunning' landscape. We look to others to help complete the picture.

References

BLOOM, B.S. (1976). *Human Characteristics and School Learning*. New York: McGraw-Hill.

KIRK, G. (1982). *Curriculum and Assessment in the Scottish Secondary School: A Study of the Munn and Dunning Reports*. London: Ward Lock Educational.

MCINTYRE, D. (Ed) (1978). *A Critique of the Munn and Dunning Reports*. Stirling: Stirling Educational Monographs, University of Stirling.

SCOTTISH EDUCATION DEPARTMENT (1977a). *The Structure of the Curriculum in the Third and Fourth Years of the Scottish Secondary School* (The Munn Report). Edinburgh: HMSO.

SCOTTISH EDUCATION DEPARTMENT (1977b). *Assessment for All: Report of the Committee to Review Assessment in the Third and Fourth Years of Secondary Education in Scotland* (The Dunning Report). Edinburgh: HMSO.

SCOTTISH EDUCATION DEPARTMENT (1980). *The Munn and Dunning Reports: The Government's Development Programme*. Edinburgh: SED (mimeo).

SCOTTISH EDUCATION DEPARTMENT (1982). *The Munn and Dunning Reports: Framework for Decision*. Edinburgh: SED (mimeo).

CHAPTER 2
School-Based Developments in Foundation English

Margaret Eleftheriou

Background

The involvement of Bankhead Academy in the Munn and Dunning developments had begun before my appointment as principal teacher of English in May 1979. Within ten days of my arrival, I had to present myself at St Andrew's House, prepared to make decisions and commitments that were to have far-reaching consequences. On that day, there were teachers from 20 different types of school; rural, urban; mainland, island; tiny, huge; deprived, well-resourced; mixed-ability, streamed; using the Certificate of Secondary Education (CSE) or not. Bankhead's contribution was distinctive because we were mixed-ability, in the forefront of CSE development in Scotland and well-equipped for resource-based learning.

The meeting proceeded at a leisurely pace; all suggestions for development work were equally welcome as this was a 'feasibility' study; it was implied that ideas were not to be blinkered by a formal and traditional approach, since we were facing a new situation in the creation of valid courses for pupils at Foundation level. We were to concentrate on syllabus and course design and not, as yet, on assessment. Bankhead's proposal to define 'Foundation' as a stage through which all pupils would pass, was seen as perfectly acceptable, along with other unusual proposals, such as the suggestion by one school that its Foundation commitment be neither more nor less than the production of a school play.

Curriculum Development and the Teacher's Role

It seemed to me, after that meeting, that the approach chosen for this feasibility study in English was one of defining objectives, designing appropriate materials and methods, trials in schools, evaluation and feedback. I did not ask myself, 'What sort of teacher-role is most appropriate to curriculum development? Employee? Or professional?' (Hoyle, 1969). I assumed that I was part of a consultative experimental process. This assumption was occasioned by the leisurely pace and genuinely inquiring spirit of that June 1979 meeting. Bankhead Academy's contribution only becomes clear when judged from that viewpoint.

Roles in Scottish Education

Scottish education is dominated by different and occasionally conflicting hierarchies whose members have allotted roles. It resembles a Ptolemaic world view, with stars and planets revolving in endless concentric spheres. Teachers, inspectors, researchers, and Scottish Examination Board (SEB) officials (another sort of luminary altogether) have their distinctive roles with universities and colleges of education winking away solemnly on the far edges of perception. Though these roles impinge upon one another, there is little interaction, as each pursues a different path towards what ought to be a common goal. Such rigid hierarchy ensures for the majority an isolation, often grandly termed independence, that fosters the traditional authoritarian pattern of Scottish education.

Given that Scotland is a small country with a compact educational structure and surprisingly little interaction, there is force in Nisbet's (1970) paradoxical conclusion that 'some changes can be introduced quickly and easily . . . for consultation takes place between people who know each other and meet frequently'.

Nature of Development at Bankhead Academy

The new session in August 1979 saw the start of several initiatives and innovations. The attitude of my departmental colleagues was of crucial importance since 'genuine innovation does not occur unless teachers become personally committed to ensuring its success' (Hoyle, 1969). In his essay, with the ironically apt title 'Innovation – bandwagon or hearse', Nisbet (1974) demonstrated that teachers do not easily accept the inevitable increase in work load, together with the loss of skills and confidence, for 'innovation de-skills'. Fortunately, not all my colleagues belonged to the Sabre-tooth Curriculum Brigade, and Grampian Region helped by providing a small amount of curriculum development time in the timetable. Suddenly new ideas sprang up everywhere: we looked at ways of producing a course to satisfy all our pupils; we examined previous work critically and new insights emerged. We looked at the four modes of reading, writing, listening and talking as a means of allowing the poor reader/learner into a previously inaccessible world. Listening stood out as virtually unknown and untried. We next looked at reading and saw that our examinations tested writing as much as reading. We devised new, contextualized assessments that tested reading skills only, as far as possible, and found that a significant proportion of our 'poor readers' were not poor readers at all; they were merely poor performers on traditional comprehension tests.

From that moment of genuine discovery, school-based development took off. There could be no reversal, for our perception of the curriculum had now changed. There could be no turning back. The metaphorical inadequacy of the language distorted the event it purported to describe. We perceived that the practices of traditional English assessment were full of unacknowledged, unsubstantiated assumptions. Our initial emphasis on the four modes led to the conclusion that language itself is the primary context of learning situations; the four modes are perceived as different contexts for learning, and are not seen in any way as discrete, or as promoting divisiveness; and this has had important implications right across the school curriculum at Bankhead.

Development at National Level

The first conference, in October 1979, showed that the tempo of development at national level had changed over the summer break. The concept of feasibility was no longer emphasized. We teachers knew it was too early to judge what might come from our efforts, because this was still only October; schools are geared to run on a yearly cycle and our cycle had just begun. The administration year is not the same shape, however, and though administrators are aware of this difference, their own short-term goals impose more urgent priorities on their procedures. Nevertheless, though progress and speed were now the keywords, the atmosphere still seemed to me to be interestingly and amiably chaotic.

Back at school the procedures and methods of trialling that we had adopted resulted in a number of visits from Her Majesty's Inspectors (HMIs) to look at our contextual reading tests, our embryonic listening exercises (a possible way into a demanding text for the slow reader), our CSE courses and the detail of our internal assessment procedures including moderation and our redrafting techniques.

All in all, a busy three months until the next conference in January 1980. Our actual commitment to Feasibility was 'Devising of new units for CSE/F using A/V stimulus and key texts – to make up several new sequenced units of work' (letter from SED dated 26 November 1979).

Assessment

Conference 2 was to concentrate on assessment with contributions from 'outsiders' on external testing procedures and formative assessment. SEB officials appeared for the first time as observers. Much interest was shown in CSE assessment methods; five teachers from three schools (including Bankhead) were quizzed in an open forum chaired by an HMI. The positive and constructive nature of formative assessment in the classroom was demonstrated; we examined CSE internal assessment procedures in the light of some trenchant conclusions on traditional marking in English external examinations and we presented evidence from our own contextual reading assessments. The Bankhead team was led to the inescapable conclusion that traditional summative assessment of English comprehension was seriously flawed. Why did we test reading skills using only a certain type of interpretation? What was being tested? Perhaps comprehension of the questions; certainly not comprehension of the passage in question.

The typical remarks put forward in professional justification of this kind of test, such as 'To separate the sheep from the goats', 'We've always done it that way', 'Everybody knows what 'in your own words', means, don't they?', 'It's in the exam, that's why!' no longer seemed trivial, but crass. As Richardson (1973) says, 'Consultation is far more complex than having a say in decision-making. It is a kind of self-education. it involves a commitment to learning that is bound to entail pain, struggle and risk.'.

Assessment of Reading

I felt as if a house of cards had collapsed, or one built on sand had begun to show cracks. What followed from that conference was very important indeed. We decided to change the nature and scope of our assessments. We had not assessed what we had claimed to assess; ergo, we had first to decide *what* we were going to assess, and then how this could best be achieved. The shape of our assessment pattern in reading changed and we decided to include material that would provide preliminary diagnostic information. This was designed to test whether we had achieved both the general aims of the unit and, since we had specified particular areas to be covered, to provide specific information about what had been learned.

Assessment of Writing

Most teachers of English acknowledge the gap that exists between the flow of creative writing within the classroom, which results in pleasure shared by teacher and pupils in a satisfactory outcome, and the set external essay, where the task is unnatural and its assessment often painfully incomprehensible and couched in negative terms. At Conference 2, attention had been drawn to the way in which even the least confident writer could improve performance by means of enabling techniques, such as the introduction of a topic by means of a picture stimulus, the spontaneous development of ideas in small group discussions or time allotted for redrafting. The idea that assessment of writing did not have to follow the impersonal form of present external procedures began to gain ground. We wondered whether it would be possible to recreate instead the friendly supportive atmosphere of a working classroom, and devise an assessment method that could bring out the best in each pupil and still yield satisfactory summative results. More HMI visits to see Bankhead's CSE examination essay in operation resulted in our adopting redrafting techniques to add to the picture stimulus and class discussion that we already used.

Assessment of Listening and Talk

Very little on listening and talk emerged directly from that first conference on assessment. The lip service paid to the importance of these elements was accompanied by an assumption that assessment in these areas was impractical. In Scotland curriculum development is almost always linked to the requirements of the external examination, which is, among other things, 'an instrument of educational policy' (Wyatt, 1973). The presence of an SEB examinations officer at Conference 2 meant that the lively exchanges on the purpose and nature of assessment did not go unnoticed in that important sphere of curriculum influence.

A combination of circumstances produced a change in attitude towards these previously 'unassessable' areas. External examination procedures were under fire; internal assessment was being examined as a viable proposition; a folio of work was to be produced for internal assessment with contents regulated by a checklist of activities stressing all *four language modes*; and since only what appeared in examinations was certain to be taught, then it seemed to be self-evident that the scope of the 'examinable' should be enlarged.

We were aware of the hollowness of flat statements purporting to promote the language skills of listening and talk, and had used these extensively to provide easy means of access to difficult texts or ideas, in our mixed ability units. Thus Bankhead was already in a position to try out some of the nebulous ideas presented for consideration.

Syllabus and Assessment in 1979–80

In retrospect, it is clear that the first two conferences were seminally important. Few restrictions had been placed on the pilot schools other than financial; the variety of the pilot schools allowed a unique cross-fertilization of ideas and practice to take place and an emphasis on the positive aspect of the SED role seemed to give grounds for hope that the ideas disseminated so vigorously would be trialled and form the basis of further development. Even so, it was well understood that there were difficult issues ahead, such as the target Foundation population, the overlap between General and Foundation levels, the balance of internal/external assessment. The tenor of the first year's work did, however, indicate openness and an attempt to reappraise traditionally held attitudes, particularly in assessment. Though it was the formative and diagnostic that were the focus of attention, it was implicitly acknowledged that external examinations could not remain unaffected in the face of changes already working their way through the system.

Change in the Nature of National Development

The honeymoon period of syllabus and assessment curriculum described above was almost as brief as the real thing. Perhaps the best way to illustrate the nature of the change that hindsight now places firmly at this point, is to provide details of what the pilot schools were coping with in general and to concentrate on one particular development, rather than attempt comprehensive coverage. Thus the teased-out detail of necessarily skimped development provides, in retrospect, a different dimension to a grimly fascinating overall picture.

Experiment in the Assessment of 'F' Courses

Conference 2 (January 1980, the busiest time of the school year) was followed by a burst of changes. A letter dated 3 March 1980 gave an alternative form of checklist of language activities (schools' courses had taken account of an *earlier* checklist). It was followed nine days later by a package enclosing experimental pupil profiles from two schools, a new draft of the National Guidelines (for syllabus and assessment) on internal assessment. One week later, further draft sections of these Guidelines on 'assessment principles, criteria, planning and techniques' appeared. It was agreed that the next session's work should concentrate on assessment, but no pattern was specified.

The new session (1980–81) had already begun when the national development plans for it were outlined in a letter dated 24 September 1980. 'The 1980/81 phase is intended to test the feasibility of a "Dunning pattern", to the extent that external and internal procedures be tried out. No particular weighting external:internal is postulated as yet, but the pattern must contain a range of possibilities, so that the relationship between external and internal measures may be examined in a practical way. This evaluation will be *statistical* and *consultative*' (my emphasis). Figure 1 provides a diagrammatic representation of what was to be piloted.

This detailed letter contained the phrase 'many elements in the external element could be criterion-referenced *not* norm-referenced' (staggering words in the light of future developments) and concluded disarmingly, 'You will note the tentative nature of these proposals and their tardy appearance – both of these matters reflect our difficulties and the highly exploratory nature of the Pilot phase.' The assessment proposals were to be discussed *one week later* on 1 October, and were to be implemented in the current session!

The Position at Bankhead Academy

For us, 'Foundation' was to be a stage through which all pupils passed and we had to decide whether to abide by our commitment and present all our pupils for assessment. There was time for only one departmental meeting to explain the highly innovatory and complex assessment proposals and decide whether it was feasible for us to continue as before. Our improved units strengthened our conviction that it was invidious to single out the low achievers as 'F' pupils. This commitment, however, entailed an assessment load of one Listening Assessment, one 10–15 minute Tape of Talk, and three pieces of writing from three different checklist activities for each of our 197 pupils. The departmental meeting lasted considerably longer than the timetabled 20 minutes but we unanimously agreed that since we were part of a feasibility study, we should make a genuine attempt to discover whether our definition of Foundation was indeed feasible.

Development in National Courses 1980/81

Conference 3 on syllabus moderation, organization and management, postponed from June to October 1980 because of union objection to further Munn and Dunning development work, was overtaken by events in assessment and our preoccupation with the new assessment proposals. Bankhead had started using listening exercises and an SEB officer visited

Figure 1

Pattern

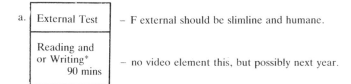

a. | External Test | – F external should be slimline and humane.

| Reading and or Writing* 90 mins | – no video element this, but possibly next year.

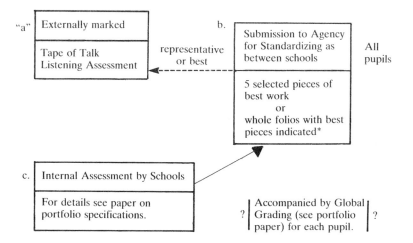

"a" | Externally marked |

| Tape of Talk Listening Assessment |

b. | Submission to Agency for Standardizing as between schools | All pupils

representative or best

| 5 selected pieces of best work or whole folios with best pieces indicated* |

c. | Internal Assessment by Schools |

| For details see paper on portfolio specifications. |

? | Accompanied by Global Grading (see portfolio paper) for each pupil. | ?

Timing

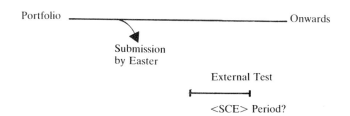

Portfolio ———————————————— Onwards

Submission by Easter

External Test

<SCE> Period?

us to see one in operation. We chose a 25-minute narrative piece, with two sets of questions, one requiring written answers, the other ticks in boxes. The text itself was rejected as too long. The second question set was approved as being more precise than the first, in establishing skills in listening.

It was then decided that four teachers from three schools (including Bankhead) should contribute to Conference 4, on assessment, two weeks later. The proposal was to have four teacher/administrator-led discussion groups, on the assessment of talk. The task was to 'bring out the criteria on which we are going to assess Foundation Grades'. By 11 November, this task had expanded to include writing and listening, and by the opening of Conference 4 on 19 November, reading had been added. The conference paper issued to help discussion was entitled 'A Guide for Assessments in English' prepared by the English panel of SEB and dated 1977.

Provenance of a Major Innovation: Grade Description

The conference paper suggested 'that before you read each of the sets of descriptions of the various grades of pupils, you mentally conjure up five pupils of your own who represent: 1 (top 10% of pupils in the year group); 2 (the next 20%); 3 (the middle 40%); 4 (the next lower 20%); 5 (the bottom 10%). Use whatever basis you normally use for your judgement.'

There followed five norm-referenced descriptions of *pupils*, presented under the headings 'Oral' and 'Written', but actually containing a full set of five grades for each of the four language modes.

I do not recall the English panel's paper being mentioned in our group discussion. We discussed talk and listening, and, in particular, criteria for grade 1 (Enhanced Foundation) and grade 2 (Foundation) awards. We decided that talk should correspond to writing in four areas of assessment, namely audibility (legibility in writing), fluency, appropriateness and communication.

After the conference the speed at which developments were undertaken was an important distorting factor in the study. There was never time to examine in detail matters on which we were being consulted, and on which decisions were being taken. This counted for little to those who saw the role of the teacher in research as 'employee'. But at Bankhead we did not share this view.

Five days after the end of Conference 4, the SEB officer who had chaired our group discussion sent me his resumé of all group conclusions. I delayed making detailed comment until 18 months later because of a host of extra commitments, including talks to a seminar for the colleges in January and for the advisorate in March, 1981 ('to talk candidly about how easy or how difficult it is to adapt a CSE syllabus to our Guidelines'). I organized the taping of 197 10–15 minute Talks on Tape, Listening Assessments (conducted in the school language laboratory) and slimline folios to meet the 31 March deadline, though we received the 'new' grade descriptions only on 2 March 1980. I also became deeply involved with trials for the research on reading and devised new 'Listening Diagnostics' for first-year pupils. I received and implemented new internal assessment procedures, was moderated for both syllabus and assessment, took part in a 'general school inspection' and spent one week of the 1982 Easter holidays at SEB as a Foundation marker.

It was at SEB in the 1982 Easter holidays that I realized that the grade descriptions had not been revised. (Hardly surprising, given the frenzied activity.) The five norm-referenced grades of pupil had been transmuted into four grade descriptions of *pupil performance*, with the insertion of the points arising from the November 1980 discussions. Norm-referenced grades 1 and 2, designed for the top 30 per cent only of the cohort, had become grade 1 (worthy of more than a Foundation award) and were therefore supposedly suitable for at least the top 70 per cent of the cohort. I now grasped that the purpose of the descriptions and their process of development ran counter to one another (perhaps an abstruse point but nevertheless significant). Their use also occasioned discrepancies of a more practical nature. The numbers game had changed: 30 per cent of the cohort had become 70 per cent. This could pass unremarked in most pilot schools but not in Bankhead where, having defined Foundation as a stage and not as a level, we continued to submit all our S4 pupils to all the assessment procedures.

I wrote my detailed comments to the SEB on 15 April 1982. They were not accepted. By then, a 'professional Group' was turning the unaltered grade descriptions into Grade Related Criteria. The existence of this group was a well-kept secret, though some of its work was revealed to the 20 pilot schools in the March 1982 'final' feasibility conference. Thereafter, further developmental work on the Guidelines proceeded along the lines familiar in Scottish education: 'The working party procedure keeps our feet firmly on the ground and there are few in Scotland who would object' (Nisbet, 1970). This is surely an example of what Chin (1971) describes as 'the use of power to alter the conditions within which other people act by limiting alternatives, shaping the consequences of acts and by directly influencing actions' and 'currently the most common form of administrative intervention to secure change'.

The Ptolemaic world-view had prevailed: I seemed so often thereafter to sound the sole discordant note in a universe of preordained celestial harmony. In March 1982 we had submitted all Bankhead pupils to the Foundation assessment and as a result in September were able to make a comparison of 'O', CSE and 'F' examination results. In late December

1982, the SEB announced that pupils would have to gain an A (Enhanced Foundation) in all four modes before obtaining an aggregated A award. Of our 91 successful 'O' grade candidates, 65 would not have obtained an Enhanced Foundation award on this basis. Even after that kind of evidence, it took some months of dissent before the proposal was shelved.

There are certain aspects of the Munn and Dunning development, however, on which I made distinctly positive comments: the central importance of the four language modes, the measure of internal assessment in the final package, moderation, the emphasis on the centrality of literature, the genuinely helpful 'teaching approaches' of the National Course Guidelines and the focus on formative and diagnostic assessment.

But the speed of the development, the unnecessary secrecy cloaking certain aspects, the refusal in certain quarters to accept unpalatable conclusions, have vitiated what might have been (and still could be) a genuine attempt to release Scottish education from the bonds of nineteenth-century patterns of thinking and behaviour. Let us hope that one of Nisbet's (1974) definitions of innovation will not be the epitaph of Munn and Dunning development in Scotland.

Cheap, meretricious and gimmicky, undertaken rashly without adequate resources to see it through.

References

CHIN, R. (1971). 'Basic Strategies and Procedures in Effecting Change.' In: HOOPER (1971), *infra*.

HARRIS, A., LAWN, M. and PRESCOTT, W. (Eds) (1975). *Curriculum Innovation*. London: Croom Helm.

HOOPER, R. (Ed) (1971). *The Curriculum: Context, Design and Development*. Edinburgh: Oliver and Boyd.

HOYLE, E. (1969). 'How does the curriculum change?' *Journal of Curriculum Studies*, 1, 2, 132–142.

NISBET, J. (1970). 'Curriculum development in Scotland', *Journal of Curriculum Studies*, 2, 1, 5–10. In: HOOPER (1971), *supra*.

NISBET, J. (1974). 'Innovation – bandwagon or hearse', *Bulletin of Victorian Institute of Education Research*, 33, 1–14. In: HARRIS *et al.* (1975), *supra*.

RICHARDSON, E. (1973). *The Teacher, the School and the Task of Management*. London: Heinemann.

WYATT, T.S. (1973). 'The GCE examining boards and curriculum development'. In: HARRIS *et al.* (1975), *supra*.

CHAPTER 3
Social and Vocational Skills: an Alternative Approach

Douglas Weir and Bob Currie

Introduction

In 1980, it became apparent to the Scottish Education Department (SED) that their curriculum development programme arising from the Munn Report (Scottish Education Department, 1977) was short of a sufficiently vocational orientation. Furthermore, the Department felt that the Munn Committee had overstated the case against multi-disciplinary courses. These two perceptions together resulted in a team from Her Majesty's Inspectorate (HMI) preparing an outline proposal for a preparation for working life course to be called Social and Vocational Skills (SVS).

This proposal, contained in an internal SED memorandum, emphasized that such a new course would have the characteristics of 'fostering those skills and attributes which will make a pupil more employable . . . be multi-disciplinary, embracing the subjects of home economics, technical education and business studies . . . be practical, and include a period of residential stay, aspects of community care, and work experience.' Because, however, the conceptualization of this, and a further two multi-disciplinary courses proposed at the same time, had not been as profound as the remainder of the Munn plan, it was considered important to provide some external research and development support for the teams of HMIs who were leading the relevant course teams.

The Research and Intelligence Unit of the SED set about identifying sources of such support and in early 1981 approached the principal author of this chapter who was then director of a development unit for youth education and training (subsequently known as the Scottish Vocational Preparation Unit or SCOVO). The approach was in terms of providing consultancy services to the three multi-disciplinary developments, and focusing particularly on developing alternative pedagogical models (process-based rather than content-based) for SVS.

The Origins of Alternatives

Negotiations

The Research and Intelligence Unit explained that SVS was emerging and that because of its novel nature, research support would be provided if an acceptable proposal was submitted. The principal author was approached because of his current interests and past experience in teacher development and vocationally-relevant education.

As the research proposal developed through various stages of drafting and discussion, it became clear that while SVS had its origins in three subject departments, an important SED consideration was whether other teachers could become involved and how they could be helped to work together across subject boundaries. While most pilot schools would use staff from the three departments, this project would use any teachers.

In addition, those developing the early models for SVS and other multi-disciplinary courses were not totally familiar with the life and social skills milieu of the Manpower Services Commission or further education courses, and would, therefore, benefit from consultancy support from researchers experienced in these areas. But it was also agreed that developmental and consultancy work would cause a degree of involvement with SVS which could obscure the researchers' perception of their influence on developments and therefore require a separate evaluation as part of the project.

Within a very few weeks the proposal had been agreed with three main strands: consultancy support for HMIs developing SVS and other multi-disciplinary courses; developmental work in up to eight schools to help a range of teachers contribute to the new course and choose appropriate teaching/learning methods; and evaluation of the developmental methods used in this project. This proposal was originally entitled 'parallel exercises' but very quickly became known as the 'alternative approach' by virtue of using alternative sources of teaching skill other than or in addition to business studies, home economics and technical subjects.

The project ran for the next three years under these three stands with the exception of the consultancy support for the other multi-disciplinary courses where the HMI teams decided that their courses were shaping up in a way which did not require the expertise of the proposers, SCOVO.

Providing Consultancy

From April 1981 the project director joined the team of HMIs responsible for SVS as consultant, to find a first draft course outline available for discussion. Over the next few months that outline went through a number of significant changes as the project director and others who joined the team brought their particular experience and perceptions to the problem of devising a course which would be attractive and relevant for parents and pupils alike.

In a curriculum development project, the role of the consultant has a number of features:

(a) By not being a member of the host organization, in this case the Scottish Examination Board (SEB) or SED, the consultant can make criticisms which those employed by the host organization cannot.

(b) If appropriately selected, the consultant will have a range of views and manner of expressing them which differ from the dominant culture of the host group and can create debate leading to reconsideration of original solutions.

(c) The views and actions of the consultant must, above all, have credibility in the host group (or its key members). This can be achieved by the consultant articulating the implicit beliefs of the host group about the areas where innovation is required and by having a visible grounding in 'real' schools and colleges where others can check the consultant's evidence.

(d) The consultant must be able to refer the members of the host group to a large reservoir of reading and contacts whenever an emerging strategy for change requires to be reinforced.

(e) The consultant must recognize that his task is not to promote one line of reasoning but to stimulate a variety of lines of development and the implementation of the one best suited to the circumstances.

The alternative project was well suited to these responsibilities because it was not committed to a narrow solution to the problems of SVS but was attempting to identify the widest possible range of means for achieving the basic aims of the new course.

By this device of consultancy support, SVS went through a number of important changes in the period up to the launch of pre-pilot work. References to a 'deficiency model' (which sees a lack of skills in young people and applies remediation) and to content drawn from discrete subject areas were removed (the latter being replaced with references to more general content descriptions of the course). Emphasis was given to the 'vocational impulse' as a motivating factor for young people from the moment of their entry to the course, and to project work with records of achievement rather than to 'subject skills' with formal assessment. The extent of the descriptions of recommended teaching approaches were dramatically increased so as to emphasize learning processes rather than teaching techniques.

Of equal importance to the manner in which the course was shaped up in the six months after April 1981 was the manner in which it was directed. In a conventional curriculum development programme in Scotland it would be common to find a group responsible for the direction which included local authority advisers, headteachers, members of the Consultative Committee on the Curriculum (CCC) committees and SEB panels. The research project argued against such representatives because they would be less likely to be directly involved in piloting and might, therefore, lack the urgency in approach and ready understanding of the classroom issues which were required if SVS was to establish itself as a credible course.

The experience of SCOVO suggested direct experience was crucial and that a new course which was anxious to reinforce certain approaches to teaching and learning should deal directly with practitioners. Instead of broadening the HMI group developing SVS, therefore, the guidelines for SVS were shared with an eclectic group of teachers, further education lecturers and industrial trainers who confirmed that the path along which the course was developing was, in their experience of working with young people, likely to be more motivating for teachers and lecturers.

The effects of the consultancy support in the early stages of SVS development were twofold:

1. Shifting the emphasis from subject content towards teaching approaches was such that many schools on entering the pilot, whether mainline or alternative, did not select staff only from business studies, home economics and technical subjects.
2. The increased involvement of teachers in the direction of the pilot was followed through from briefing meetings (June 1981) to national conference (November 1981) to the aftermath of the conference where teacher interpretation of the course purpose was such that the only logical next step was to incorporate SVS school coordinators in the HMI development group (January 1982).

Having reached that stage, the first phase of consultancy was over and the main emphasis moved to maintaining this momentum, mainly by supporting the project schools. The difference between them and other pilot schools was no longer primarily in the subject background of their SVS staff (since some teachers of business studies, home economics and technical subjects were involved in the alternative schools), or in the teaching approaches being used (since an agreed set of teaching approaches had emerged from the consultancy work), but in the relationship with project staff and in the interaction among and within project schools.

The Alternative Approach

Purpose

One of the main intentions of the project was to explore the issue of integrated studies as raised in the Munn Report and illuminate it. The Munn Committee (SED, 1977, para.5.5) examined the claims for integrated studies but was not convinced by them.

> . . . Firstly, it has been maintained that integrated studies make possible the use of more effective teaching methods, since they are less dependent on the heavily didactic or authoritarian approach which is said to be associated with subject teaching . . .
>
> Secondly, it has been maintained that integrated studies constitute a better way of motivating pupils, since they involve not so much the acquisition of specialist knowledge as the exploration of themes and topics directly related to the pupils' own concerns . . .
>
> Thirdly, it has been maintained that integrated studies enable teaching to foster such capacities as problem-solving, enquiry, hypothesising and critical thinking . . .
>
> Fourthly, it has been maintained that integrated studies make for better relationships in schools and classrooms . . .
>
> The common weakness of all these arguments against subject teaching is that they confuse the principle of curriculum organisation with other, logically independent principles.

Enlisting the Schools

All schools entering the SVS pilot were nominated by their regional authority. The research project did not interfere with this process except to suggest to certain schools showing an interest in the purposes of SVS that they might volunteer for nomination.

Once schools were nominated (16 from 1981–2 and a further eight from 1982–3) the HMI leading SVS and the project director agreed on an appropriate distribution so that the project obtained its quota of schools adopting the alternative approach (four and two respectively). That distribution took account of school size, geographical location and knowledge of the school's reputation in being open to new ideas.

By this process the 'alternative' schools emerged as a group with as diverse interests and backgrounds as the totality of SVS schools. Furthermore, because of the consultancy impact of the project, they were subject to the same constraints and requirements as other pilot schools.

HAROLD BRIDGES LIBRARY
S. MARTIN'S COLLEGE
LANCASTER

Making the First Contact

The 'alternative' schools were visited by the researchers, and the nature of the alternative project, and their proposed involvement in it, were discussed with the headteachers. It was made clear what the commitment would involve for access to pupils and staff by the researchers, and release of staff for in-service training and meetings. After a full discussion, and time for second thoughts on both sides, the schools were offered the options of withdrawing from the project, or committing themselves to it. None withdrew, although at this stage there was some scepticism and unease in relatively conventional schools about the impact of this innovation on the rest of the school and in relatively innovative schools about the constraints on their freedom of action brought about by participation in an SED pilot exercise.

The premises on which the researchers based this negotiation with the schools were that the alternative approach to SVS was designed to make progress towards:

1. more diversity in the instructional process;
2. a shift in emphasis from transmission of knowledge to organization of the pupils' learning;
3. individualization of learning and a changed structure in teacher–student relationships;
4. an acceptance of greater cooperation with other teachers in schools and a changed structure of relationships between teachers;
5. working more closely with parents and others in the community, and maximizing the use of new sources of learning in the community;
6. accepting a diminution of traditional authority in relation to children and towards more involvement in community life.

The direction was therefore towards breaking down the barriers between the classroom and the community, and changing the teaching and learning procedures within the classroom. This broke the notional line management relationships in schools by spreading responsibility for the course more widely, sometimes even beyond the school, and broadened the role of the teacher from the autonomous expert within the classroom to the facilitator of a wide range of experiences. It was crucial, therefore, to have headteacher approval. For some schools 'alternative' SVS could have been seen as a radical 'power to the teachers' approach and likely to cause friction within the school. But by spending time briefing the headteachers and subsequently keeping them fully up to date with developments, the project was more likely to be protected from such friction.

Identifying the Coordinator

A multi-disciplinary course has no obvious locus within the departmental structure of a school. It was therefore necessary to ensure both that someone had a specific responsibility for the course and sufficient status to lend 'clout' in such matters as timetabling and resources allocation. In providing this opportunity for senior staff to be involved in innovative cross-disciplinary development, the SVS feasibility study anticipated certain aspects of the HMI Report on secondary school management (SED, 1984a).

> The posts (AHT) concerned with the curriculum have not achieved their potential . . . The autonomy of subject departments has proved to be a barrier to the influence of the assistant headteacher, and has put a brake on the development of whole-school curricular policies. The pace and complexity of current development are beginning to force on schools a reappraisal of the curricular functions of assistant headteachers (para.4.2.11).

> . . . The success of current developments depends heavily on the contributions of individual teachers, and it falls to school management to ensure that suitable contributions are being made (para.5.1.11).

In trying to reconcile these two aspects of effective coordination and responsibility for groups of teachers the project made another contribution to the development of SVS. The initial view of the project team had been that no hierarchical relationship was required within the SVS group of teachers, but it soon became clear that some formal link was required with senior staff of the schools and with the overall pilot which could be accomplished through a member of the senior management staff in schools. The project resolved its own dilemma by encouraging these coordinators to become teaching members of the SVS course thus being in a position to talk from a basis of first-hand knowledge about SVS when involved in 'external relationships', and working with other teachers on an 'equals' basis in the course itself. This was successfully accomplished.

Convincing the Teachers

A start had to be made at classroom level by establishing the roles of the researchers and the teachers. Fullan (1972) has drawn attention to evidence that the users of innovations frequently did not understand the ideas and principles underlying what was being proposed, so that they could not explain in any specific way the key aspect of the innovation. It was the concern of the researchers that from the beginning this should not apply to the alternative project. The strategy therefore had to be one which avoided any implications of 'expert' or 'hero-innovator' in the role of the researchers. This is particularly important in education, where we are dealing with people (teachers) whose stock-in-trade is knowledge and understanding.

Early contact with the teachers, therefore, took place in their own schools, and where possible in their own classrooms. For the researchers, the role of listener was pre-eminent, and such information- providing as was necessary to introduce the course took the form of sharing a common problem on how to cope with it, rather than 'I'll show you how this can be done.' Although adopting this relatively low profile, non-expert stance, it was still necessary to establish credibility in the eyes of the teachers. The researchers were soon asked 'where did you teach?' and perhaps more pointedly opportunities were found to confront them with classes of pupils. This ranged from the formal, 'Maybe you could talk to the kids about SVS tomorrow' to the instant, out of the blue, 'The class are in next door, just now – do you want to meet them?'

Only after this crucial stage of establishing credentials was it possible to start the process of innovation rolling, and then the procedures adapted were designed to reflect the mutual trust which had been established. Elliott (1981) has pointed out that:

> In action-research 'theories' are not validated independently and then applied to practice. They are validated through practice.

He goes on to develop Lewin's basic cycle of 'Identifying a General Idea' which 'cannot be fixed in advance, but should be allowed to shift'; 'Reconnaissance' which 'should involve analysis as well as fact finding, and should constantly recur in the spiral of activities, rather than occur only at the beginning'; 'General Planning'; 'Developing the first Action Step'; 'Implementing the first action step' which 'is not always easy, and one should not proceed to evaluate the effects of an action until one has monitored the extent to which it has been implemented'; 'Evaluation'; 'Revising the General Plan'; then spiralling into the second action step, and so on.

The role of the researchers, therefore, became that of participating in a continuous process of reviewing ideas in practice, in the light of that practice clarifying the problems and questions which arose, and assisting in the reframing of the ideas so that they could be implemented. This implied a two-pronged strategy of observing and participating in the work of the schools, and of providing the means for the teachers to come together away from their schools, with time to consider the evidence of the 'Reconnaissance', and to decide on the next step forward.

The Project Activities

The School Visits

To preserve links with schools and maintain good relationships with senior staff, each visit to an 'alternative' school gave some time to meeting the headteacher and coordinator. Such meetings, however, created a number of risks: the researcher might be used as a 'spy' on the SVS teachers, the 'cosiness' of the headteacher's study might create a rhetoric about the progress of SVS which was not consistent with its practice and the project might be distracted from its real purpose of working directly with teachers and pupils.

Throughout the alternative project, these dangers were borne in mind and it was one area in which the strategy of having two researchers was advantageous. Since one of these was the field worker and therefore most susceptible to pressure from senior staff of the school, the project director occasionally used a tactic of distancing himself from the classroom. By this tactic he could negotiate with senior staff, and talk through problems which seemed likely to obstruct the course work.

School visits, then, centred on discussions with the course coordinator, observation of and participation in the learning process with teachers and pupils, and contributions to staff team meetings. Each of these provided a different perspective on how the course was being operationalized within the school, the first tending to produce what we have called the 'rhetoric' of the course, or how it was planned, the second the relationship between planning and practice, and the third a consideration of how the school's interpretation of the course related to developments elsewhere in the project. The researcher's role in the alternative project was thus both to feedback to the teachers an account of what he saw to be actually happening in the learning situation, and to stimulate discussion on how this related to the centrally conceived aims of the course. All of that was accomplished by having two researchers of different background and style to perform the separate roles of 'critic' and 'friend' for each other and for the schools.

The Meetings – For Discussion

The alternative project did not see meetings of the staff involved as information-providing structures or in-service training sessions which were separate from the main business of what was happening in the school or indeed as 'perks' to get staff away from their regular routine for a day. Instead, they were regarded as an integral part of the development strategy. A way had to be found, therefore, to avoid the 'special, one-off occasion' status, and care had to be taken to ensure that the teachers could see the meetings as 'theirs' rather than occasions when they would be asked to perform under the direction of some external body or person. Ownership of the project had to stay firmly with the teachers, and not shift when meetings were held on someone else's territory.

The strategy adopted was consistent with the non-expert stance which the researchers assumed generally, and consisted of using the school visits to identify the needs and concerns of teachers and the meetings as occasions when there would be sufficient time away from the immediacy of the classroom for all concerned to work through the problem.

In this model, it becomes critical that the researcher is able to identify the real, sometimes underlying, concerns of the teachers, and, as well as a great deal of trust, an open interviewing technique is essential. For this purpose, written returns, questionnaires, etc., are useless, as they merely encourage stilted, non-self-revealing responses. As Piaget (1979) says in criticizing the questionnaire as a means of obtaining access to a person's mental processes:

> But the real problem is to know how he [the subject] frames the question to himself, or if he frames it at all. The skill of the practitioner consists not in making him answer questions but in making him talk freely and thus encouraging the flow of his spontaneous tendencies instead of directing it into the artificial channels of set question and answer.

The researcher's job therefore becomes the identification of problems and blocks in the development, and the re-stating of these in a way which will allow the teachers to grapple with them. In a project dealing with a maximum of six schools and with never more than 24 teachers involved, it was relatively easy to use such a research strategy. When everyone can meet in the ordinary room rather than a large lecture theatre, ownership is more easily assumed by the whole group.

The Meetings – For Preparation

The collective meetings served a second key purpose – using the 'alternative' group as a spearhead at conferences and meetings of all pilot schools. The 'alternative' schools could have remained aloof from the rest of the pilot, experimenting exclusively with teaching approaches. This was certainly a tendency which some of the 'alternative' teachers would have followed due to a common suspicion of 'authority' (headteachers, local authorities, HMIs, CCC and SEB) among teachers. The outcome of the project's consultancy work, however, had been to blur the distinction between the 'alternative' schools and the rest of the pilot (the 'mainline'). If the 'alternative' was then to make a distinctive contribution to the development of SVS it had to be through participating fully in the whole pilot programme, and the support of the project team and the opportunity for regular meetings (both of which other schools were denied) provided the occasion for rehearsing tactics which could be used at conferences and, later, at coordinators' meetings.

The Meetings – For Course Development

Some of the 'alternative' meetings were single day and others were two or three day residential. Particularly in the latter, it was possible to formalize the 'alternative' approach and prepare strategic initiatives. Two such initiatives emerged from the 'alternative' meetings: the nature of the course and the processes of learning. These were successfully fed in to the main pilot.

The first initiative (September 1982) arose from a concern that the course lacked a multi-disciplinary identity and still described its objectives in skill development terms which were close to existing 'subject' definitions. Through a residential meeting the approach to the SVS course was redefined in 'Have Taken Part' and 'Can Do' terms which subsequently became the 'Learning Experiences' and 'Learning Outcomes' of the final course.

The second initiative (March 1983) arose from a concern to leave as little room as possible for any teacher, 'mainline' or 'alternative', to fall into conventional teaching approaches. By this time the distinctions between 'mainline' and 'alternative' were reducing almost to the point of extinction and so the initiative was likely to fall on fertile ground. As with the learning outcomes, the results of this exercise were influential on the feasibility study as a whole, forming as it did the basis for the 'Teaching and Learning Approaches' section of the SVS national Standard Grade Arrangements (SEB, 1984b); a section which thus far is unique in SEB documents of this kind. That the influence is real and not illusory is further confirmed by the inclusion of these principles as part of the moderation requirements for the course, thus ensuring that the process element is not relegated to obscurity now that the course has been disseminated nationally.

Coordinators' Meetings and Pilot Conferences

The rapport and trust developed in 'alternative' schools' meetings had a further pay-off when staff from these schools joined those from the other pilot schools at coordinators' meetings and pilot conferences.

The alternative group, by the influence of the project team, had a common identity and a sense of purpose. These led to a more constant membership and regular pattern of attendance than other schools. Furthermore the experience of working together fostered a greater understanding of the course, more confidence in putting a case forward and better skills in dealing with complex issues in a large group. All of these attributes were used in participating in larger gatherings, in contributing to working groups, and in demonstrating to all other schools that the alternative group had ideas which would work, which would make SVS distinctive and which were worth imitating. Ultimately, therefore, the alternative group became acceptable, the whole pilot came together and the model course was used as a baseline for the final version of SVS. This version, although formally formulated by a Joint Working Party of the CCC and SEB, was significantly affected by the activities of the research project.

Review

Consultancy

In the context of a curriculum project, an influence on the direction of the development is crucial otherwise a sense of ownership quickly disappears, and the traditional 'just tell me what you want me to do' attitude reasserts itself among teachers. One of the aspects of the project which teachers most consistently quoted as useful was the consultancy role of the researchers as 'insiders' in steering groups and official bodies. In the beginning, this was seen as useful in gaining access to information on a personal level rather than through the 'officialese' of paper communications. As the project developed an identity, the value was seen in the reverse flow of information and ideas (from practitioners to the centre), and it was essential that the project team worked with the teachers to ensure that the ideas coming from the teachers had an influence over the development of the pilot. By the end of the project, access to decision making was more direct, as the teachers themselves took on responsibilities as members of working groups and the SEB panel and as regional and national moderators for the Standard Grade awards. The image of the researchers as 'influential', however, persisted, and it will be interesting to observe how the motivation and involvement which has been such a feature of the project survives, once this feeling of having a 'voice on the inside' is removed.

Networking

The strategy of working with a small group of schools and small groups of teachers allowed the researchers quickly to build up a close, supportive relationship. Regular contact with the researchers, both in schools and in out-of-school meetings, enabled teachers themselves to be mutually supportive, and to establish relationships of trust which offered a more open sharing of problems. It was useful, nevertheless, for the researchers on occasion to act as a complementary 'critic–friend' team, rather than combining the two roles in one person, in order to stimulate innovation either in the groups or in individual schools. It is interesting that at the final meeting of the project teachers, this aspect of the researchers' behaviour was referred to as 'creative deviousness', awareness of its existence being expressed as 'knowing something was going on, but not quite sure what'. This awareness did not, so far as we are aware, harm the mutual trust relationship.

Potentially more important than the relationship with the research team, however, was the growth of a self-generating network between the schools. This became evident after the first 'Thursday to Saturday' residential meeting, when there had been time to break down personal and professional barriers and become increasingly independent of the researchers. Whether this network will survive the withdrawal of central support remains to be tested. This would depend on the various roles adopted by the researchers either being replicated from within the group, or becoming redundant now that the course had evolved from a gleam in the developer's eye to a lusty infant. If it is to survive, the course must, like all infants, be capable of existence separate from its parents, no matter how much they may wish it to remain dependent.

Acceptability

The final recognition of the way in which the alternative approach infected the whole pilot is found in the SVS Standard Grade Arrangements document (SEB, 1984b) which serves teachers as the 'code of practice' for SVS. It highlights the multi-disciplinary nature of the course and the importance of teachers' personal qualities as well as their subject expertise in fulfilling the course's aims.

> Social and Vocational Skills is not a distinct subject, but is, rather, a course or a curricular approach. As such it does not readily find a place in a conventional school curriculum with its structure of independent subject departments. Moreover it is not considered feasible that any existing subject in the curriculum could, within the subject boundaries,

embrace all the aims of Social and Vocational Skills. The solution to both these problems has been sought in the adoption of a multi-disciplinary approach. This approach enables teachers more readily to stand aside from the basic tenets of their subjects, and see their contribution to the course from the perspective of the needs of the pupils and how they, as teachers, might meet these needs by drawing on their personal skills, interests and attitudes as well as their subject expertise . . .

. . . Any teacher, irrespective of subject discipline, can contribute to the course, perhaps by developing new contexts and applications for the subject specialism, certainly by placing great emphasis on personal skills, interests and attitudes . . .

. . . The alternative approach of using teachers, regardless of subject discipline, has the obvious advantage that potentially very many more teachers are available to implement the course. Not only does this make the course less susceptible to the difficulties caused by changes in personnel but it also provides increased organisational flexibility. In addition, there are more opportunities for interested teachers to be involved. A drawback of this method is that if none of the teachers is from the practical subjects, some aspects of the course can be harder to undertake, either because of difficulty of access to suitable accommodation or because of lack of familiarity with some of the practical processes and equipment . . .

. . . Practice is beginning to show that it is not a simple choice between alternatives; many schools in both parts of the pilot programme are using a combination of teachers from practical subjects and teachers from other disciplines. All schools have, however, come to see the benefits of a multi-disciplinary approach.

Conclusion

SVS has maintained most of the focus outlined in the introduction to this chapter. The influence of the alternative approach is identifiable, however, in a number of ways.

In the first instance, it is now well-established that any teacher can contribute to the course since it is not dependent on any particular subject expertise.

Secondly, the process nature of the course is well-represented in the greater emphasis on learning experiences than on learning outcomes, in the way in which course moderation highlights that course plans can be amended during the two years of the course according to teacher experience and pupil need, and in the heavy stress placed on negotiation between teacher and teacher, or between teacher and pupil.

Thirdly, the relevance of the course in curricular and in pedagogical terms is demonstrated by the rapid move from 24 pilot schools in 1983 to almost half of all Scottish secondary schools (over 200) offering the full Standard Grade course in 1984. Teachers have valued the opportunity to work with pupils in a more informal and less didactic manner, and pupils have valued the opportunity to learn in 'real life' situations.

Although piloting was reduced by a year, primarily because of the accelerating demand at governmental level for technical and vocational courses, and although assessment requirements had to match the remainder of the Standard Grade programme, the models of participative development sponsored by the style of action research used in the project and adopted by the national development, have been robust enough to attract many schools to offering SVS and to suggest a key role in curriculum development for courses of this type.

Much of this chapter and the full account of the relevant research project will be found in the publication by the same authors, entitled *The Responsibility of the Teacher* (Scottish Vocational Preparation Unit, 1985).

References

ELLIOT, J. (1981). *Action Research: a framework for self-evaluation in schools.* London: Schools Council.

FULLAN, M. (1972). 'Overview of the innovative process of the user', *Interchange*, 3, 2–3.

PIAGET, J. (1979). *The Child's Conception of the World.* London: Routledge and Kegan Paul.

SCOTTISH EDUCATION DEPARTMENT (1977). *The Structure of the Curriculum in the Third and Fourth Years of the Scottish Secondary School (The Munn Report).* Edinburgh: HMSO.

SCOTTISH EDUCATION DEPARTMENT (1984a). *Learning and Teaching in Scottish Secondary Schools: School Management.* Edinburgh: HMSO.

SCOTTISH EXAMINATION BOARD (1984b). *Standard Grade Arrangements in Social and Vocational Skills.* Dalkeith: SEB.

SCOTTISH VOCATIONAL PREPARATION UNIT (1985). *The Responsibility of the Teacher.* Glasgow: SCOVO.

CHAPTER 4
Teacher Collaboration in Multi-Disciplinary Courses

Pamela Munn

The Courses

One of the distinctive features of the government's curriculum development programme for 14- to 16-year-olds in Scottish secondary schools was the introduction of multi-disciplinary courses. On the surface, these courses represented a radical alternative to teaching and learning because they were offered explicitly as experiments in a programme which endorsed the single subject as the basic unit of study. The courses were heralded as new and different from single subject courses, although the precise nature of their distinctiveness was not made explicit. The national guidelines for each multi-disciplinary course gave its aims and objectives in general terms, recommended structures for course organization and management, outlined the kind of teaching approaches which would be appropriate and identified the broad 'fields of study', 'modules' or 'themes' which the course would encompass. The substantive content of the courses, the kinds of knowledge with which they would be concerned and the kind of collaboration amongst teachers which would be appropriate were areas, at least initially, of teacher responsibility.

Three multi-disciplinary courses were included in the development programme. They were, Health Studies (HS), Contemporary Social Studies (CSS) and Social and Vocational Skills (SVS). Each course was envisaged as requiring collaboration among teachers from three subject departments. The departments contributing to HS were home economics, biology and physical education. History, geography and modern studies contributed to CSS. Home economics, technical and business studies contributed to SVS. An alternative approach to SVS, taking teachers 'best able to fulfil the course objectives regardless of department' (Scottish Examination Board, 1984) was adopted as an action research project at the same time as the subject-based approach. The courses were planned as two-year courses, and in the first instance were piloted at Foundation level only. Foundation was the most basic of the three levels at which the courses were offered. The successively more demanding levels of General and Credit were excluded from the pilot exercises. Although it is now policy to offer the courses at both Foundation and General, they will lack the prestige of certification at Credit, a fate not shared by single subjects.

The full pilot exercise began in 1982–83, and involved 60 schools spread throughout Scotland. The courses followed developments in English, mathematics and science and were in advance of developments in the single subjects contributing to the courses. This timetable had some advantages for multi-disciplinary developments. It clearly gave them a headstart and an opportunity to become established in the school curriculum at a time of general upheaval in curriculum provision. It also meant that in the pilot schools subject teachers' energies could be unambiguously directed towards multi-disciplinary course development rather than diffused across developments at Foundation, General and Credit in their individual departments. Biology teachers, however, could find themselves involved in piloting both in Foundation Science and in Health Studies.

Against these advantages of the timing of multi-disciplinary course developments, however, might be placed teacher anxieties about the implications of the early introduction of such courses for the future of their own subjects. Some teachers were worried about the future existence of their subjects on the school curriculum, especially given falling rolls. Others such as home economics staff were worried that their subjects might be transformed out of all recognition because of · involvement in multi-disciplinary courses.

The context in which research on teacher collaboration was undertaken, therefore, contained several interesting features. First, there was no central prescription about the kind of collaboration teachers were to adopt. Given Scottish teachers' unfamiliarity with multi-disciplinary courses and their subject specific orientation, we were interested in their interpretations of the meaning of a multi-disciplinary course. The evidence from the few such courses in existence in Scotland, such as integrated science, suggested that interpretations were in terms of collections of discrete subject components. Would this be the pattern adopted in the new multi-disciplinary courses? Secondly, the curriculum development approach moving away from a centre-periphery model towards one of partnership between the teachers on the one hand, and the centre on the other, was an unfamiliar one to many Scottish teachers. Few of the teachers involved in the research, for instance, had participated in a national curriculum development exercise in which guidelines on course content were at such a general level. They were accustomed to the detailed syllabuses accompanying nationally certificated courses from the Scottish Examination Board (SEB) and to devising their own individual courses for non-certificate pupils. In only a few instances where regions such as Lothian and Grampian have permitted pupils to sit CSE Mode III, had teachers had any experience of developing a syllabus for external moderation. Thirdly, there were mixed feelings amongst teachers about the introduction of multi-disciplinary courses in advance of single subject developments.

The Research

The research focused on four HS schools, three SVS schools and two CSS schools. The schools were visited twice, first in 1982–83 and again in 1983–84, when they had had more experience of the courses. The time spent in each school was used to interview teachers involved in the courses, to observe formal and ad hoc collaborative processes at work, multi-disciplinary lessons and 'typical single subject' teaching.

Given the absence of any theoretical model of collaboration to be tested empirically and the explicit encouragement of teachers to adopt whatever collaborative approach seemed most appropriate to them, the research operated on a minimal definition of the term. It defined collaboration as involving communication and negotiation and set out to explore who communicated and negotiated with whom, about what and under what circumstances. The aim of the research was to try to identify factors affecting collaboration both in the individual multi-disciplinary courses and more generally across all three courses. The interest in factors affecting collaboration directed attention to questions about how decisions were reached about the courses, the role of subject expertise in decision making and incentives towards collaboration. There was no predetermined list of factors whose effects were to be tested. Data were analysed by progressively building up categories from the original research questions. In this way, a profile was developed of the collaboration teachers adopted and of the factors affecting collaboration.

Collaboration

The research revealed an immense variety in approaches to collaboration within and across the nine schools. It would, however, be a mistake to identify a number of fixed models of collaboration with the implication that these were mutually exclusive. The picture is one of almost constant change with different people, subject-matter and procedures involved at different times and in response to different circumstances. By presenting a profile of teachers' experiences, others interested in multi-disciplinary developments may be alerted to the kinds of collaboration appropriate for them.

Who Collaborated With Whom?

All the nine schools had identifiable multi-disciplinary course teams consisting minimally of a teacher from each of the contributing departments and a course coordinator, usually a senior member of staff. Coordinators ranged in status from headteacher to head of department, although most were assistant headteachers. Some schools included guidance and/or remedial staff in their teams. The collaboration was primarily amongst the team members. There were, however, some instances of attempts to involve outside agencies in courses, local employers, health visitors, and local war veterans, for instance, and one school had involved a community service volunteer.

Teachers involved in multi-disciplinary courses rarely communicated with other non-involved members of their department about them. It was even rare for teachers in the same department, but teaching different year groups on a multi-disciplinary course, to collaborate with each other.

Communication and negotiation with the school staff as a whole about the course was haphazard. Indeed, one or two incidents were observed where staff not involved in the courses were annoyed at the removal from their lessons of some pupils on an out of school activity associated with the courses. This was particularly the case with SVS. Its emphasis on learning through participation in activities such as community events, or work experience, or residential stays, implied imaginative timetabling to avoid such problems.

How Did Collaboration Take Place?

Not all schools found it possible to arrange the recommended regular meeting time for their multi-disciplinary course team. Some teams met during the lunch hour or after school, but generally found this to be unsatisfactory. On the other hand, where team meetings were timetabled not all team members might be able to attend. In some instances they were timetabled to be with classes or were used to cover a class for an absent colleague. The larger the team the more difficult it was to arrange a meeting time. In addition to, or in place of, regular meetings, school teams collaborated in an ad hoc way, when walking along the corridor to lessons, travelling together in the same car, or using the staffroom at the same time. Clearly, ad hoc collaboration of this kind seldom involved all team members. Sub-groups formed and re-formed over the course of a school session. There were times in the school year, however, when it was easier for teams to meet. This was particularly the case during the summer term and public examinations, when teachers lose senior classes, and, in Scotland, are not involved in public examination invigilation. More recently, in-service time has been provided by regional authorities and this has created opportunities for teams to meet. Lastly, collaboration could take place through team teaching opportunities which could be used either as a vehicle for ad hoc discussion or as powerful non-verbal means of conveying to team members one's views on the teaching approaches appropriate for the course.

What Did Teachers Collaborate About?

The extent of collaboration on any particular matter varied enormously both within and across the schools. All the teams collaborated to some extent on course content, but this could range from a general discussion about the number and title of topics to be taught in a year, to joint course writing. Similarly, teams collaborating on assessment could mean all team members together assessing the same work done by pupils or agreeing to award a grade to pupils on the basis of fairly global judgements on their ability. It was relatively rare for teachers to collaborate on teaching methods and more likely to happen in schools where there was provision for team teaching either within or across departments. Resources were another matter involving collaboration. Again collaboration on this might range from a casual reference from one teacher to another about the existence of, say, a book or film strip, to joint viewing of a video or film spilling over into discussion about how to use the resource most effectively. There had been little joint course evaluation. Again, however, one can envisage different approaches to this varying in depth and specificity. Finally, all teams had collaborated to some extent on the organizational arrangements for the course. These included the pupils to be involved, whether to adopt a bloc rotation system amongst the contributing departments and the details of its operation, and the allocation of money for the courses amongst team members.

Teachers tended not to collaborate about the meaning of the multi-disciplinary nature of the courses and the kinds of knowledge with which the courses were concerned. The emphasis was on the immediate problem of what to teach, not on the way in which the courses were different from single subject teaching or on the ways in which the various single subject contributions might be welded into a coherent course. Indeed teachers in HS and CSS consistently demanded a more detailed syllabus and clearly prescribed content. Given the lack of time to develop their own materials and the multiple demands on teachers' time, the materials used were frequently little different from those used in the past with less able pupils. It was not unusual for teachers to complain that they would have to re-vamp their single subject courses for the less able as they were using the same material in multi-disciplinary courses. The main differences teachers mentioned were those of assessment and certification.

In SVS the situation was rather different. Although teachers' initial reaction to the course could be to divide it into subject specific components and use worksheets which they had always used, the tendency was to see the course as at last providing something worthwhile for the less able pupil. They saw it as different from single subject teaching with less emphasis on the didactic transmission of knowledge from teacher to pupil and more emphasis on the teacher as a facilitator or partner in experiences from which both teacher and pupil would learn. The compulsory pupil experiences contained in the course could be an effective mechanism for promoting collaboration not only on course content but on its purposes and the kind of knowledge with which it was concerned. Planning an old people's Christmas party, for instance, could provide coherence to inputs from business studies (issuing invitations, costing), home economics (food preparation, laying tables) and technical (making direction signs for the event). Pupil experiences could also be used as a vehicle for promoting negotiation between pupil and teacher about the kind of experience to engage in and as a stimulus to reflecting on what had been learned.

Dimensions of Collaboration

The teachers' experience suggests that no one approach to collaboration will be appropriate over the whole two years of any of the multi-disciplinary courses. There were occasions when whole school teams felt it necessary to meet regularly, such as when overall course planning was discussed or when assessment procedures had to be drawn up. On other occasions sub-groups of two or three team members met to plan the detailed content of particular pieces of work or to discuss particular resources. It is this diversity of approaches to collaboration that suggests it would be helpful to identify the dimensions of collaboration rather than mutually exclusive models. Six dimensions are suggested by the schools' experiences.

1. Organizational arrangements for collaboration are clearly important in determining who collaborates with whom. Teachers could ask themselves how many classes would be feasible; how many teachers would constitute the team; whether they want meeting times structured into the school timetable; whether they want opportunities for team teaching and so on. Many of these kinds of questions may not be in the teachers' power to resolve. Where there are opportunities to influence timetabling, however, it is important that teachers are aware of the

impact on their collaboration which the school timetable can have. School management should also be aware of this.

2. Related to organizational arrangements, but distinct from them, is the dimension of availability of staff for the multi-disciplinary course. In organizational arrangements the concern was with numbers of staff and pupils involved and the timetabling of the course. Here the concern is with the availability of subject staff and the kind of role the course coordinator might play. Teachers could ask themselves questions about whether it is necessary to have subject expertise from each of the contributing departments available throughout the course or for particular parts of it. Could the course be taught by one teacher with 'guest appearances' by particular subject experts? What kind of role is it appropriate for the coordinator to play: administrator, developer, teacher?

The remaining dimensions of collaboration concern what teachers see as appropriate to collaborate about. Running through these dimensions is the question of the purpose of the course in terms of the kind of learning the course is trying to promote and the nature of its distinctiveness from single subjects.

3. Course content figured in collaboration in all the nine schools involved in the research. Teachers might ask themsleves if they want to collaborate on this at a general level or engage in joint course writing. On the occasions when teams or sub-teams saw joint course writing as necessary, they spoke of it enthusiastically and as better than courses they had produced on their own.

4. Course evaluation is a dimension of collaboration related to course content but separate from it. Very few school teams had engaged in evaluation, feeling the pressure of work to be on producing course materials rather than on reviewing the materials produced. A question for teachers engaging in collaboration, then, is whether they see joint evaluation of their materials as necessary or desirable.

5. Pedagogy emerged as a dimension of collaboration. It was possible for teachers to collaborate on course content and not about how they were intending to teach the content. It may be that under pressure to develop materials for multi-disciplinary courses teachers took for granted their existing teaching skills as appropriate for the courses or perhaps as qualified and registered teachers collaboration on teaching methods was regarded as unnecessary. Whatever the reasons, teachers involved in multi-disciplinary courses might consider whether they need to collaborate on teaching methods.

6. The final dimension of collaboration is that of assessment. In the second phase of school visits, more demands were inevitably being

made on pilot schools from the SEB as dates for implementing a new system of assessment drew nearer. Clearly an important feature of any course is the way in which and the criteria against which pupils are to be assessed. In multi-disciplinary courses teachers have to decide how they are going to approach this and the amount of detailed collaboration amongst the team it requires.

The wide variety of interpretations of the meaning of collaboration in multi-disciplinary courses thrown up by the research suggests that there is no ideal approach for all teachers in all circumstances. Instead, it has been suggested that there are a number of dimensions of collaboration, that teachers need to pay attention to these, and ask themselves questions about the most appropriate form of collaboration for them.

Factors Affecting Collaboration

In deciding what kind of collaboration is most appropriate for them, what kind of factors affecting their collaboration do teachers need to consider? The one factor mentioned by every teacher was that of time. Teachers stressed the competing demands on their time and the ordering of priorities that had to take place if they were to function at all. The multiple demands on teachers meant that they universally welcomed some mechanism such as a meeting time which created space for collaboration. The frequency and length of such meetings are clearly matters for schools themselves, but unless there is some mechanism to bring teaching staff together, it is likely that multi-disciplinary course collaboration will be swamped by other activities. Blocs of time for developing course materials were also of vital importance during the early stages of a school's involvement in multi-disciplinary courses.

The perception of the role subject expertise had to play in materials development also impinged upon collaboration. Where teachers saw a particular topic as falling 'naturally' within the subject competence of a particular teacher, then collaboration on content was at a fairly general level. The relevant subject expert was left to produce materials on his or her own. Where teams agreed that the course did not require particular subject expertise or that a topic did not fall naturally into the province of a particular subject expert, then detailed collaboration on content and indeed joint course writing were more likely. Interestingly enough, all the teachers said they were willing to teach material which was outside their subject knowledge. It was preparing and creating new materials where reservations were expressed. There were reservations too about managing practical lessons using 'foreign' equipment.

Team relationships were viewed by teachers as important for

collaboration. It was necessary for teams to get to know one another and for members to get on with one another if collaboration were to be successful. It is impossible to define the ingredients necessary for good relationships, of course. Most teachers mentioned it as something that they saw as potentially important, with most teams describing their relationships as 'good'.

The geography of the school can affect collaboration. Where teachers all use the same staffroom, or teach in classrooms near to each other, or share the same workbase, then informal, ad hoc collaboration is easier. Schools with several buildings and separate staffrooms clearly do not promote informal contact.

What of incentives towards collaboration? Again, there were distinctions between the SVS teachers on the one hand and CSS and HS teachers on the other. While all teachers welcomed the courses' focus on less able pupils, SVS teachers tended to describe pupil reaction more positively than HS or CSS teachers. They were also more positive about the future of SVS. CSS teachers raised doubts about its future, given developments in history, geography and modern studies. Similarly, some HS teachers wondered whether the course was duplicating content available elsewhere in the curriculum. There were differences, too, in perceptions of the school-based nature of the course. SVS teachers saw the course as *theirs* in a way that HS and CSS did not. For a discussion of these differences, see Munn and Morrison (1985).

Implications for Implementing Multi-Disciplinary Courses

One of the major implications for implementing these courses is the decisive influence of the school timetable on collaboration inside and outside the classroom. The timetable can provide opportunities or not for teachers to meet, to team teach, to take pupils out of school and to make guest speakers a feasible proposition. Bloc timetabling was generally regarded as preferable to individual 35- or 40-minute periods. The preferences of teachers in multi-disciplinary courses, however, have to be set alongside the preferences of other teachers who may not share the same views. Imaginative timetabling is a major prerequisite for the successful implementation of courses which require both collaboration and a substantial element of out of school activity.

Secondly, the choice of coordinator is likely to have a major impact on the success of these courses. Where schools are given the freedom to develop their own materials, the need for someone to take charge of this process is clear. There needs to be someone to encourage development, share the workload amongst staff, deal with all the paperwork and to liaise between the team and various others inside and outside school. Whether that person need be or indeed should be a senior member of staff is a question for the schools concerned. In only two schools did coordinators at senior level find it possible to be actively involved in teaching and development and thus to play the kind of role in the courses which most staff would have preferred.

A clear area for the attention of a senior member of school staff, on the other hand, is in the overall coordination and planning of the 14 to 16 curriculum. As schools have begun to implement the courses which have been developed, areas of overlap of content have begun to emerge. There are such areas amongst the three multi-disciplinary courses as well as between a particular multi-disciplinary course and single subject courses.

In this context it is vital to consider whether multi-disciplinary courses are indeed trying to make a distinctive contribution to pupils' learning. If they are seen as no more than collections of separate subject contributions, watered down from 'O' grade content, what of their future survival? Certainly they could have an administrative rationale in the sense of providing a more efficient use of staff than running separate single subject courses at different levels. They might also be welcomed by teachers as a way of sharing out the teaching of the less able that they are going to have to do in any case. On the other hand, the courses have to exist in schools organized in subject departments and in a country where teachers are trained and registered as competent to teach in particular subjects. The courses are not available at Credit level whereas single subject courses will be. On educational as opposed to administrative criteria, survival of the courses must largely depend on their ability to offer something different and distinctive from single subject teaching that is worthwhile to pupils and teachers.

SVS has tried to establish its distinctiveness in its perception of knowledge as something pupils acquire by reflecting on their experiences. This is reflected in distinctive classroom processes, involving pupils in negotiating course content and encouraging pupils to accept responsibility for their own learning. Teachers' interest and enthusiasm for the course, reflected in their organization and participation in a range of outside school activities, the preparation of materials and the formation of a national association of SVS teachers may well indicate that despite the differences in status from single subject courses and the demands of collaboration, at least one multi-disciplinary course is here to stay.

References

MUNN, P. and MORRISON, A.T. (1985). *Approaches to Collaboration, in Scottish Schools, in Multi-Disciplinary Courses, 14–16.* Stirling: Stirling Educational Monographs, University of Stirling.

SCOTTISH EXAMINATION BOARD (1984). *Standard Grade Arrangements in Social and Vocational Skills, at Foundation and General Levels.* Dalkeith: SEB.

CHAPTER 5
Learning to Discuss – a Teaching Approach

Thomas R. Johnson

Introduction

The Case for Discussion Programmes

During the late 1960s a growing body of opinion began to question the traditional model of teaching. It suggested that pupils, within the classroom setting, should be given greater opportunity to communicate more freely both with teacher and peer group. As a result of this the 1970s saw discussion programmes, ranging from those developed by teachers to those organized nationally, being initiated.

The supporters of this innovation argued that the primary benefits arising from the development of discussion programmes would be twofold, first at an individual level and secondly at a national level (Bridges, 1979). Individuals, they claimed, would improve their ability both in verbal communication and discussion, and in doing so would develop in confidence, perception and the ability to listen. This in turn would enhance their interest and attitude towards the subject. Secondly, it was felt that an improvement in the individual's ability to communicate would result in greater involvement and participation within our democracy. Therefore such courses would ultimately be of national benefit.

The Problems of Discussion Put Into Practice

During the 1970s I, like many of my colleagues, was impressed by the apparent credibility of the foregoing arguments and became interested in developing classroom discussion techniques. Departmental programmes, for all years, were gradually introduced. These ranged from teacher-controlled discussions and pupil initiated, small group discussions, to various types of role playing exercises. An invitation to present one such programme for first- and second-year secondary pupils

(S1/S2) to the Lothian Region Modern Studies Annual Conference, some four years ago, appeared to endorse our apparent progress.

However, throughout the years of devising, revising and attempting to assess these programmes, whilst convinced of the desirability of the selective use of discussion programmes, our modern studies department was confronted with recurring questions and problems.

For example, the programme seemed 'hit or miss': it worked with some classes and not with others and a small number of individuals in the group soon emerged as the main contributors and dominated proceedings. How would those who contributed very little to discussion be helped? Did enthusiastic noise mean success? The ultimate question was, 'What are we trying to develop, the pupils' ability to communicate or their understanding of the course content?'

Our answer was that we wished to develop both content and conceptual understanding of the subject, in addition to improving pupils' communication abilities. It seemed a plausible answer but it was the last four words, 'improving pupils' communication abilities', that exposed our inadequacy when we made some attempts at assessing verbal communication in our S1/S2 programme. The many difficulties we encountered saw us retreat to the widely held view that pupils must have derived some communicative benefit from being exposed to discussion experiences even if we could not recognize it.

It can be seen that this view still persists widely and the attempts to use discussion in both the Munn and Dunning (14 to 16) and the 16 to 18 development programmes have posed problems for teachers. In introducing some of the new courses, there has been a failure to make clear what is meant by and implied by the new emphasis on verbal communication and teachers have little experience which is relevant. In consequence, they are being asked to promote and even assess parts of programmes for which they have no training. However, such a training is presently available.

An Opportunity for Training

In the autumn of 1981 the Lothian adviser for modern studies invited me to join a pilot course in discussion skills for interested teachers from Lothian Region English and modern studies departments. The organizer of the Discussion Skills Project, Eileen Francis of Moray House College of Education, conceived it in response to an initiative from the Scottish Education Department (SED).

Originally the idea was to commission a 'discussion-skills package' which could be used by teachers in conjunction with the newly structured curriculum generated by the Munn and Dunning proposals. However, as the college pilot course progressed it soon became apparent that producing a universally adaptable 'package' would be impossible; as the complexities of group discussion and group management became apparent to us, so too did the fact that normal teaching conventions and methods would not be appropriate to instigate such a 'package'.

The rest of this chapter is devoted to describing the process that caused my perception of group work to change and helped me to develop my ideas about discussion. I present it in three phases. First, I consider briefly the developmental phase which is concerned with the personal development of the teachers involved in the Moray House project. Secondly, I offer a detailed commentary on the experimental discussion programme developed for use in the classroom. And thirdly, I discuss some points relevant to the dissemination of this approach to teaching among the wider community of teachers.

Discussion: the Development Phase

There were two parts to this phase: a person-centred approach and a skills-centred approach. In the first part, the project group of teachers met for ten sessions each of one-and-a-half hours in Moray House College. The aims of the initial 'person-centred' model of training were to create an awareness of the group as a social system, to recognize the processes which shaped the group and to encourage the development of empathy, through insight into group behaviour. We became aware of these aims as Eileen Francis enabled us to look at group process issues and relate this to teacher and pupil roles inside the classroom. For a comprehensive description and explanation of this model of training see Francis (1982). The ten-week course proved to be a catalyst in that it awakened our understanding of group process which was essential in preparing us for the next part of our development.

In the second part, the 'skill-centred' approach, our main tasks were, first, to identify the component parts that comprise a 'good' discussion and secondly to work on methods and materials that could be applied in the classroom. This resulted in the creation of a programme which will be described in the next section on the Experimental Phase.

The Development Phase can be summarized by saying that the project group of teachers, through experience of analytical group work and self-directed learning, began to develop their own process thinking abilities. From this emerged two important aspects of our work:

1. A growing ability to observe group process and to facilitate effective discussion.
2. An identification of the individual skills involved in small group discussion.

Our contact with Moray House College remained essential in the development of the discussion programmes we were to attempt in our own classrooms.

Discussion: the Experimental Phase

The Stages

The development of our experimental programme was in two stages. The first stage monitored the programme under controlled conditions. Third-year pupils, from the school of another member of the project team, made eight weekly visits to Moray House during which time they were filmed as they progressed through the programme. I had the role of observer/process consultant.

Although the setting was very different from a normal classroom situation we gained valuable insight into the validity of the programme. For myself, the experience exposed my limitations as a process consultant. The constructive criticism I received was very helpful to my preparation for the second stage.

The second stage introduced the programme into a normal classroom setting. The major concern of finding a school willing to fit our programme into an existing syllabus quickly evaporated when in the summer term of 1982 my headteacher allowed the 'Learning to Discuss' programme to become a part of the S2 'general rota' (i.e. a space in the curriculum which at that time was shared or rotated among economics, religious education, music and discussion skills). This opportunity gave us the freedom to continue experimenting with the programme without fear of hindering a content conscious course.

The pupils on this S2 rota excluded those of top academic ability leaving an average class size of 28. The description of their programme will be necessarily brief and this does to some extent detract from understanding the purpose and application of some of the exercises. I again would recommend reading *Learning to Discuss* (Francis, 1982). However, there are some aspects of the programme that are of crucial importance and I will describe these in some detail before discussing the role of the teacher and assessment.

The Programme

We devised a sequence of ploys and exercises that were designed to illustrate and help teach each of the component parts of discussion. These were:

1. Oral Skills Training
2. Introducing Group Work
3. Organizing
4. Attending
5. Contributing
6. Non-Verbal Contributions
7. Responding and Learning New Roles

For *Oral Skills Training* various games were used to demonstrate the significant elements of listening and speaking. Pupils were also introduced to self-assessment methods as a means of identifying their problems and progress.

In *Introducing Group Work* it was necessary to have a flexible seating arrangement. Rooms with fixed seating are unsuitable for achieving the desired small group formation. This 'desired small group formation' was achieved by those pupils who, through trial and error, demonstrated for themselves the fundamentals necessary for allowing discussion to take place, i.e. they must have easy access to the group to allow them to speak without raising their voice, listen without straining and see each other with minimal head movement. The best formation, they concluded, was a circle. Once learned and reinforced pupils used this knowledge outwith the 'discussion' classroom.

We then, collectively, defined the word 'discussion'. A typical definition would be that 'Discussion can only take place when group members are allowed to express opinions and ideas, to make comments and question each other, freely, without inhibition or fear of embarrassment'. This enabled us to identify the purpose of the course which was to focus on the personal development of the pupil and not the development of the teacher's course content. This groundwork was very important in allowing pupils to visualize the task ahead and thus be ready and willing to participate in the training.

The *Organizing* exercise was aimed at increasing pupil awareness of group organization when given a set task, e.g. to calculate the height of the group members. On completion of the exercise they described their perception of group organization.

Our session on *Attending* attempted to enable pupils to discover that every group member had a valuable contribution to make and that completion of a task was dependent on the involvement of all group members. The session took the form of a detective game. Pupils were given 'content prompts' in the form of clues in order to solve the various aspects of a murder. Each pupil was responsible for their clues and only they could read them to their group. *All* the clues were needed for the solution of the murder.

Before experimenting with this exercise I believed academic ability would play a large part in its successful completion. There is no doubt that one or two group members need a good agility of mind, but it is interesting to record that a group of academic adults failed to complete the exercise after an hour whereas the average time for a 2nd-year class was 25 minutes with the record being an incredible eight minutes.

With the completion of this exercise even the normally silent group members began to realize that their contributions were important and that the more dominant members were being forced to listen to them.

Two key issues were identified for presentation in the *Contributing* exercise:

1. How can the contribution rate of the submissive and reluctant group member be improved?
2. How can those high contributors who dominate the group be encouraged to say less and thus be prepared to listen more?

With these considerations in mind a controlled experiment was undertaken to test our hypothesis that:

Group members with similar contribution rates perform most effectively when working together.

The stages of the experiment were as follows:

(a) Each group discussed two set moral problems.
(b) Each group member recorded the contribution rate of all members of the group including themselves.
(c) The teacher made recorded observations, mainly measuring contribution rates in each of the groups.
(d) A contribution rate chart, based on the combined observations of teacher and pupils was made.
(e) New groups were formed on the basis of similar contribution rates.
(f) Contribution rates of the new groups were measured.

The evidence was consistently clear that pupils with a similar contribution rate performed most effectively when grouped together for discussion. Those in the high contribution group revelled in the challenge of working in their new group and regularly commented that 'it is much harder work'. Those in the other new groups enjoyed being rid of the high contributors. This was especially true of the lowest contributors who, without exception, were always very positive about their new group.

This change of group was, for them, very important for the following reasons:

(a) For many of these pupils it was the first time that they had been given the opportunity both to speak and be listened to in a group discussion.
(b) These pupils no longer adopted a submissive role but were prominent in the completion of group exercises.
(c) There was a marked rise in their contribution rate.

In conclusion, this often-repeated experiment showed very clearly that manipulation of group membership had a crucial effect on the member's contribution rates. This evidence must call into question the belief that pupils will improve their skills in discussion merely through increased exposure to discussion whether it be among the whole class or in small groups. Whilst some pupils may gain in confidence and in their ability to speak (not discuss), it is more likely that existing group roles will be reinforced, i.e. the dominant will continue to dominate and the submissive will continue to contribute little or nothing.

However, affecting contribution rates was not an end in itself as we then had to capitalize on the pupils' changing perceptions of their role in group discussion. The pupils remained in their newly formed groups as the skill training began in earnest.

The main purpose of the *Non-Verbal Contributions* exercise was to encourage the use of eye-to-eye contact. Such contact from this point became standard practice in all the subsequent exercises. It was no coincidence that the low contributors found this very difficult. It was a great step forward, for their confidence, when they began to develop occasional eye-to-eye contact.

Responding was a crucial element in the programme and a considerable time was devoted to this session. The exercises were designed to develop the ability to listen to a group member and to respond, in a variety of ways, to what they had just said.

First, pupils were encouraged to prefix responses (process prompts) by stating, e.g.

I agree with so and so when she said..
I didn't understand...
Do you mean ....when you said...........................

Pupils practised statements and responses which, when collectively grouped, formed what we called a Pattern of Interaction.

To use this pupils were numbered (no two consecutive numbers adjoined each other) and each was given a copy similar to the abbreviated example shown below.

Number 1 – Expresses an opinion
   2 – Responds by expressing areas of agreement or disagreement and adds further comment
   3 – Asks a question about No. 2's further comment
   2 – Responds
   4 – Introduces a new idea
   5 – Responds as No. 2 did
   6 – Asks No. 4 a question to clarify their new ideas and so on. The pattern can be as long as is deemed necessary.

I usually ended with the following two summarizing roles.

   3 – Expresses their opinion stating how much agreement and disagreement they have with the other group members
   5 – Tries to summarize the position of the group.

Although the ensuing discussion was initially very contrived, with practice, it soon became more natural. However the main purpose was for pupils to recognize the tasks that gave them the greatest difficulty and thus practise them in subsequent exercises.

The S2 rota time allocation always expired by the time we reached the latter stages of the 'responding' sessions. We were left, therefore, with insufficient time to investigate one important area. We would have preferred to have carried out a controlled investigation into the effects on pupil group behaviour of grouping them once again on a random basis. However, in spite of this shortcoming, we have been greatly encouraged by pupil response to the programme which will be described in the next section.

Teacher Role and Assessment

The teacher's classroom role assumed a new identity as we now saw the teacher as:

(i) The conductor organizing, coordinating and preparing pupils for participation in the discussion activities.
(ii) The process consultant conducting discussions about the pupil's discussion both during and after the task was completed, facilitating the giving and receiving of feedback on the effectiveness of the discussion process and identifying problems which might be managed differently in future discussions.

Further to this second point, it must be emphasized that it was of vital importance that pupils did not become dependent on the teacher as the only observer of process and were allowed sufficient opportunity to identify group behaviour for themselves.

Part of the teacher's role was that of assessment. The procedure of recorded teacher and pupil observations was used in three separate areas of assessment:

1. Course evaluation;
2. Diagnostic assessment;
3. Pupil evaluation.

The course evaluation was particularly subjective. The teacher wrote a report after every meeting with the class. This report was then available for future reference both for himself or herself and, if required, for consultation with Moray House College. It attempted to assess the value of the exercise and to make general comment on how the class had adopted and managed the tasks.

Although our original method for *diagnostic assessment* lacked sophistication in its presentation, it nevertheless succeeded in highlighting the problems of both the individual and the group. The method used, at the end of every exercise, was to question pupils as to their progress both as an individual and in their relation to the group. Pupils who had difficulty with extended writing were encouraged to give short responses sometimes aided by word banks or sentence completion suggestions. Pupil perceptions were essential to supplement teacher observations and their combination often led to individual counselling.

One of the easier, least complicated examples concerns a fairly academic pupil from a newly formed, low contribution rate group. When asked for written comment about progress in her new group she stated that she was finding the change difficult because it was the first time ever that she had found other group members willing and keen to listen to her. She explained that in all her previous group experiences, in primary school, secondary school and even with peer groups, she was always interrupted when trying to contribute but now given an attentive audience she felt tongue-tied and embarrassed.

This particular problem was straightforward and the pupil was able herself to identify lack of confidence as the cause of her problem. The remedy we tried was for her to practise timed-speaking, at home, looking into a mirror. She was to keep the teacher informed about her perceived progress. The pupil, with admirable dedication, tried the various home exercises and soon began to feel that she was improving. This story emphasizes the significance and importance of a skill-centred, process-conscious course. Despite the problem being obvious, the fundamental communication difficulty experienced by this pupil is common to many in their formative years. Schools have consistently failed to develop a systematic approach to help remedy such problems.

Towards the end of the programme a *pupil evaluation* of their course progress was undertaken. In this the pupils commented on the value of the course to themselves as individuals. A consistent pattern of response emerged not only from the original class but from subsequent classes as well. The main improvements they recorded were in:

1. Ensuring an appropriate group formation.
2. Confidence in speaking (especially low contributors).
3. Willingness to take part in discussion.
4. Eye-to-eye contact.
5. Ability to listen.
6. Willingness to speak more openly and honestly.

Perhaps the two most satisfying kinds of comments that emerged have been: first, the claims made by many pupils that they have used their developed skills outside the 'discussion' classroom with their peer groups, in their homes and in other classrooms when discussion takes place (a few observant staff have confirmed this); and secondly, the admission by virtually all the pupils that although initially they thought discussion would be a 'skive' in the end it turned out to be hard work.

Comment

We are under no illusion as to the 'real' success of the programme. First, society has not been designed to allow the convenient separation of high and low contributors. Therefore what we must aim to achieve is an understanding of group process so that we may encourage the more confident, high contributors to listen more and the more submissive, low contributor, to gain more confidence and exhibit some of the skills necessary to help them take part in discussion. We do not claim that the programme will give everyone equal ability.

Secondly, the programme is not an end in itself. It would be ludicrous to claim that after eight weeks of this course S2 pupils will have completed their development in discussion skills. All we can justifiably claim, is that within the duration of the course pupils respond well and through experiential learning can identify improvements in their personal development both as a communicator and as a group member. Ideally, what is required is a whole-school policy that will, throughout the pupil's school career, allow process analysis to be observed when discussion takes place.

In order to achieve this, however, process thinking development must receive a wider teacher audience and it is to this matter that the final phase is devoted.

Discussion: Consolidation and Expansion

Although I hope I have helped in a small way by writing this chapter and by giving numerous talks to a wide variety of audiences, it is the service offered to Lothian Region (and beyond), by Moray House College, that has provided the platform for the expansion of interest now taking place.

In the latter half of 1982 a resource base for the Discussion Development Group (DDG) was established in the college. The work of the DDG has been further consolidated by the recent appointment of a research associate. It provides college-based in-service programmes which offer staff experimental group work of the kind described earlier in the chapter. These are supplemented by a consultancy service for teachers developing group work in schools and a resource centre for teachers wishing to develop skills in discussion group work. Incorporated in the centre are a library and video facilities that can be used by visiting teacher and pupil groups. External in-service training programmes have been successfully offered to staff in a number of schools and colleges covering three different regions, and the provision of 'programme illumination' has been undertaken on numerous occasions to a variety of interested groups and bodies.

This service offered by Moray House reflects the growing interest and recognition given to this field of work. This continued growth is essential to create the network of training, support and materials necessary to sustain the present momentum and to allow progress in developing a greater understanding as to the value of verbal communication programmes. Areas such as 'learning through discussion' and the creation of 'whole-school' policies can only be more fully explored when there is a greater knowledge and understanding of process development. To attract this wider audience, however, would demand a considerable change in attitude: 'education' would have to rationalize its purpose and priorities thus identifying, and giving recognition to, essential personal developmental skills; verbal communication would have to have a place as one of the priority skills, i.e. a structured place in the school curriculum; in-service training for staff would have to become more widely available and be both financed and encouraged by the SED and the local authorities; colleges of education would have to introduce, as an integral part of student training, in-service courses on discussion.

These comments may appear extravagant in their demands but if 'education' is serious about implementing radical changes for pupils, then staff must be ready and able to respond to the new challenge. New methods and ideas require 'new' thinking and approaches and it is to this end I hope I have begun to stimulate an interest in the 'Learning to Discuss' programme.

References

BRIDGES, D. (1979). *Education, Democracy and Discussion.* Windsor: NFER Publishing Co.

FRANCIS, E. (1982). *Learning to Discuss.* Edinburgh: Moray House College.

CHAPTER 6
Mastery Learning in Context, Theory and Practice

Eric Drever

Origins of the Research

It is an interesting coincidence that while in America Benjamin Bloom was concluding from his researches on mastery learning that

> Most students become very similar with regard to learning ability, rate of learning, and motivation for further learning – when provided with favourable learning conditions (Bloom 1976)

in Scotland the Munn Committee was deciding that

> . . . curriculum design has to allow for the fact that abilities differ widely over the school population and within each age-group (Scottish Education Department, 1977:19)

and was recommending that to cope with these differences in ability three different levels of curriculum were needed in the middle years (S3 and S4) of Scottish secondary education.

Our own research had convinced us that 'ability' played a much less important part in determining pupils' success in learning than was conventionally believed (Drever, 1982). We had stopped thinking in terms of 'general ability', as a quality intrinsic to the pupils and of which each had a different, fixed amount. Instead, we had come to think of each pupil's 'specific abilities': the collection of things that he or she knew and could do at any particular time.

This led us to propose an investigation into Bloom's claim that

> . . . we can now speak of the learning conditions which can bring about equality of educational outcomes for students . . . at very high levels of attainment (Bloom 1979)

We did not suppose that Bloom's approach could be transplanted in detail, nor that conditions or attitudes in our schools would make them readily receptive to his ideas. We did not therefore see the project as a test case along the lines of 'does mastery learning "work"?' Rather we saw it as a study of feasibility at a fundamental level. What form might Bloom's ideas take in a Scottish context? Could our teachers think in this way about pupils' abilities, and act accordingly?

The new courses for S3 and S4, being designed on Munn's assumptions about differences in ability, had already avoided Bloom's most challenging claim, that we can provide for 'equality of educational outcomes . . . at very high levels'. Besides, we could expect these courses to follow on from a conventional curriculum in the first two years of secondary education (S1 and S2) in which a back-log of half-learnings and low expectations of success had accumulated, creating exactly those conditions which Bloom describes as unfavourable to learning.

We proposed therefore to work in S1 and S2, and to study teaching and assessment across several subjects within a curriculum embodying Bloom's ideas. We found in St Margaret's High School a fairly typical West of Scotland comprehensive in which there was a school policy commitment to Bloom's ideas, and where the staff had already begun to develop their version of mastery learning in the curriculum for the first two years.

Our interest lay in what teachers themselves could achieve within realistic constraints, and so we left control of the development entirely with the school staff. They were involved in many other projects both local and national (and in phasing out corporal punishment). We negotiated with the school a collaborative action research strategy which allowed us to be helpful without interfering, and to develop an understanding of the ways in which the teachers themselves made sense of things.

The Idea of Mastery Learning

We found it necessary to begin by dispelling some popular connotations that mastery learning had acquired, including a quite counter-productive emphasis on dramatic results ('four-fifths of students can achieve what less than one-fifth achieved before'), and notions either of a mechanistic resource-based programme with infinite series of remedial worksheets, or that 'mastery learning is just what the good teacher does anyway'. We defined it as 'teaching that is based on Bloom's explanation of school learning'.

The traditional view of school learning is illustrated in Figure 1 (p.60). We expect a wide variation in pupils' *attainment*, and we 'explain' this as the natural consequence of pupils having different amounts of *general ability.* But how do we know that they differ in ability? As a rule we infer this from the differences in attainment. The 'explanation' is no explanation. But what it does is important: it allows us to take for granted the quality of our *instruction.*

Figure 1

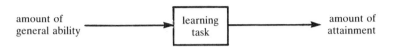

amount of general ability → learning task → amount of attainment

In our interpretation of Bloom's model (Figure 2) we abandon the idea of *general ability* in favour of *specific abilities.* A pupil's chance of success on a learning task will depend first and foremost on whether he or she has already learned the specific skills and knowledge that this task requires. (It also depends on whether he or she has an *interest in learning* from the task, and on the adequacy of various *aspects of instruction.*) The various attainments that result from the task add to his or her stock of specific abilities, thus raising the chances of future successes.

Given conventional teaching, pupils with a large stock of abilities will usually have the prerequisites of a task, will generally be successful, and will add to their stock. Others whose stock is initially small cannot add to it, and so fall further and further behind. Bloom's model thus explains the patterns of performance that we observe at present, but without invoking the traditional view of ability, as something intrinsic to the pupil and beyond our influence.

Figure 2

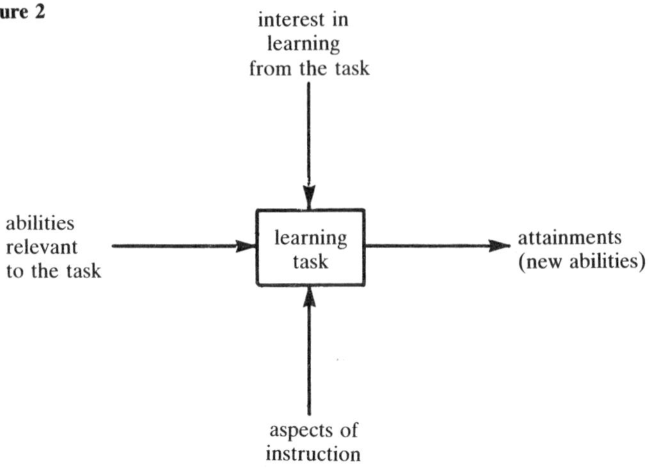

interest in
learning
from the task
↓

abilities
relevant → learning task → attainments
to the task   (new abilities)

↑
aspects of
instruction

Instead, Bloom offers an optimistic view of what is possible. Since, in principle, the prerequisite abilities for each task *can be taught*, we could, in principle, arrange things so that no pupil would attempt a task without them and all would learn to a high level. Our research has not caused us to doubt the value of his ideas, though it has confirmed the immense difficulties involved.

For example, to develop a system of assessment that is adequate to support a mastery learning approach requires three major steps.

1. First, instead of the 'dipstick' approach in which we take any sample of attainment to be an index of *ability,* we have to describe in useful detail what each pupil has and has not mastered. This alone requires a fully criterion-referenced approach.
2. We then need to explore why a pupil may have failed to learn, so that something may be done about it. This implies diagnostic assessment, again in a very full sense of that term.
3. Only then can we develop ways of assessing pupils *before* instruction, against the known prerequisites of each task. This is what mastery learning logically requires, but even Bloom's work has not aspired to.

Our research also shows that barriers to Bloom's ideas arise because so much of current pedagogy and organization is dependent on the traditional view of ability. Both kinds of problem, practical and ideological, are illustrated in the following accounts of work within the project.

Mastery Learning in Practice: the School Report

By the start of our research the school had already adopted a form of report which eliminated traditional marks and grades. Instead, each pupil's performance was reported at one of three levels of mastery, in relation to each of four elements of each subject.

However the teachers' committee steering the development was aware of problems. Some people were still thinking of 'levels' as points on a sliding scale of general ability, as grades and marks had been before. There was disagreement about which 'level' should correspond to the 'core' that every pupil was to master, and about how that core should be defined: as 'what we know they can master' or as 'what we would like them to master'?

To help the teachers understand the problem, we presented a paper, in which we quoted an example from another school, where the method of reporting appeared inconsistent with its attempt at a 'mastery' approach.

core mastered + all extensions   = A
core mastered + some extensions   = B
core mastered (first time)   = C
core mastered (after remedial work) = D
core not mastered   = E

Here, though the majority of pupils had mastered the core curriculum (everyone with D or better) the report looked as if it was based on a traditional grading system, and emphasized only the differences in performance.

We argued that this would inevitably occur if the core curriculum was seen as a 'lowest common denominator' that even the least able could master. In that case the main interest would naturally shift to the amount of extension work done. If however the core was seen as a worthwhile challenge for all pupils, even the most able, then people would want to report on the core work in some detail.

These discussions led to a new form of report, in which only one 'level' was identified: mastery of the core. Teachers were required to write comments on any areas in which this had not been achieved, and a description of the elements of the core was provided separately. This showed willingness to eliminate the 'sliding-scale' approach to assessment and to identify common goals for all pupils in S1/S2.

However the definition of the desired core of attainment still faced both practical and ideological difficulties. We had argued that pupils, parents and teachers saw 'worthwhile challenge' mainly in terms of 'O' grade certificates, and we had suggested that the core in S1 and S2 must include all the specific skills and knowledge thought necessary as prerequisites for beginning certificate work in S3. In that case, any pupil who was reported as having mastered the core in a particular subject could expect to enter the corresponding 'O' grade course.

This was not acceptable. One practical reason was that teachers could not specify the 'prerequisites' of 'O' grade courses. This was not surprising since entry to these courses has traditionally been determined on estimates of general ability and not by pupils' attainment of specific skills.

But teachers were also chary of being held accountable for the 'O' grade success of all the pupils who might perform satisfactorily in S1/S2. They forced us to recognize that within a strictly hierarchical and contracting system in which talk of compulsory teacher transfers and school closures is common, Bloom's optimistic claims can be used as much to threaten as to inspire, and that this can be a major obstacle to them being tested seriously.

The further paradox is that once the teacher has accepted responsiblity for his or her 'O' grade class, it is exactly the kinds of clear (though *educationally* limited) targets provided by public examinations that are dealt with skilfully, in ways not unlike mastery learning. It is not yet clear that teachers (or anyone else, Bloom included) can achieve something similar in relation to notions of general education.

Mastery Learning in Practice: Coping in the Classroom

The commonest approach to mastery learning that we found in the school was based on a 'core and extensions' curriculum with built-in 'diagnostic' tests. In this the class began each unit with several lessons of 'core' work. Then, after a formal test, pupils had one or two sessions of 'remedial' or 'extension' work depending on their individual scores on the various parts of the test. Some of the science teachers became interested in improving 'diagnosis' by using more flexible, informal tests. We helped them to interpret the pupils' errors on these tests, and found four main categories of mistakes:

1. misunderstanding something at the time it is taught;
2. understanding it at the time but forgetting it later;
3. understanding it but confusing it with something taught later;
4. miscellaneous 'slips'.

It was clear that mistakes in the first three categories ought to be identified and remedied at the time when they arose. This emphasized the value of having short tests during each lesson, and (for mistakes of types 2 and 3) pointed to a need to include, systematically, some earlier material in each test to check for 'forgetting' and 'confusion'.

In practice this was not too difficult to do. Teachers could set their own short-answer tests at the end of lessons and go over it with the class, relying on this discussion to put right most of the random errors there and then. They would also note which pupils got several questions wrong, and which questions several pupils got wrong, as a basis for further investigation and more systematic revision and remediation during the next lesson. The teachers claimed several advantages for the approach:

(a) the pupils performed better;
(b) the pupils quickly learned the purpose of these tests and liked them;
(c) the teachers learned much more about why pupils made mistakes;
(d) the system was far easier on teachers than what one described as 'four weeks of ordinary lessons and one week of chaos'.

Some interesting points arose from this work. First, to let the teacher make up the question, and the pupil make up the answer, seemed to provide better diagnostic information than the use of ready-made multiple choice questions. The reasons why pupils made mistakes were also illuminating, the commonest being absence when something was taught. This had gone unnoticed when using formal diagnostic tests (and of course, throughout years of traditional teaching). We found that when pupils made a mistake, they tended to repeat it later, and this suggested that remedial measures are not so important as ensuring sound learning initially. (This in turn supports Bloom's emphasis on pre-empting failure by paying heed to the prerequisites of learning.)

Modern languages teachers had also reported problems with diagnostic testing in the areas of speaking and listening skills. Despite being told that these tests were meant to help them learn, pupils still saw them as a protracted ordeal, as something 'done for the teacher' and which could result in the stigma of failure. The teachers sought to remove that stigma, to make pupils take responsibility for their own learning, and at the same time to reduce the time spent on reteaching and retesting those who failed. To do this they prepared a checklist for the pupils and went over this thoroughly in class, getting pupils to assess themselves and mark areas where they felt they were weak. Pupils were then organized into groups to work on these weaknesses.

The teachers reported exceptional performance on subsequent tests, and better motivation not only towards the tests but towards the usually tedious business of revision. And the complete process saved two whole sessions which would normally have been given over to the grind of retesting and reteaching disenchanted pupils.

In both these classroom experiments, teachers had found evidence of the improved motivation and performance that Bloom promises.

Mastery Learning in Practice: Remedial Education

Right from the start of the project one question arose repeatedly: what proportion of pupils can mastery learning cater for? The question stemmed from a long-running debate in the school about the provision of remedial education. In a paper for the teachers' steering committee, we analysed the problem in relation to mastery learning, and to current policy on *Pupils with Learning Difficulties* (Scottish Education Department, 1978).

Bloom's view seemed clear: all normal children were mentally capable of learning what the schools had to teach them, and to a high standard, but only when they brought to a task the prerequisite knowledge, skills and interest. When these conditions were not met, we could expect pupils to experience 'learning difficulties'. If pupils were broadly lacking in the general prerequisites for secondary work and in particular for the S1 'Mastery' curriculum, then it seemed that a special 'Remedial' programme might be needed to teach them these things before they could embark on S1 with any chance of success.

Once again we met the practical problem that teachers were unable to state the prerequisites of their courses with any precision, referring only in a general way to 'literacy' and 'numeracy'. This was only to be expected. Working within the traditional view of school learning, teachers need to be expert on the targets of learning and on knowing whether pupils are or are not achieving them, but they have little experience of thinking about the range of knowledge and skills that secondary work in general depends on and assumes, or about the specific abilities that pupils do bring to that work. They do not need to think in that way, because in the traditional view, learning difficulties can always be 'explained' as stemming from poor 'general ability'.

However, the current official thinking on learning difficulties at national and regional levels seemed more compatible with Bloom's in its emphasis on problems arising from the mis-match between curricular demands and pupils' existing repertoires of specific abilities. We found that school policy and the teachers individually spoke about pupils in three categories, which corresponded broadly to the discussion in the HMI's report, and which we could translate into Bloom's terms:

(a) pupils with 'severe difficulties', so generally deficient in cognitive and affective prerequisites of S1 work that their chances of success on most learning tasks would be slight;
(b) pupils 'at risk', with a back-log of weaknesses which could, however, be removed by constant diagnosis and remediation within a normal mastery learning programme;
(c) the typical pupils, any of whom at some time might find 'learning difficulty' with a particular task.

The pupils identified by the school as in the first two categories also gave us an account of their own difficulties which had much in common with Bloom's. They seemingly did not doubt that they could learn if the conditions were favourable, and they reported needing and seeking specific task-related help which was difficult to come by in a full-sized class. And so they 'got stuck' (their term) and had less *time-on-task* (a key Bloom concept) than the others. The notion of *general ability* was not salient in their account, though it might be in their teachers'.

Nevertheless, the suggestion that the first group with severe deficiencies might need a one-year 'bridging' course before S1, to provide them with the skills basic to secondary work, was ideologically quite unacceptable to teachers, although admitted to be consistent with mastery learning principles. They talked about the stigma of segregation, or the cruelty of demanding too much of these pupils, or their own belief that these pupils would benefit in some unspecified way from the S1 courses. Bloom seems unaware of such possible issues, and so offers only limited help in resolving the problems of remedial education.

Some Conclusions

Bloom Revisited

Our research has shown up inadequacies in Bloom's model of 'school learning'. He emphasizes that the factors affecting successful learning are 'alterable variables', within our control, and he presents a convincing case for believing that if we prevent errors from occurring and accumulating then all our pupils can learn to a high level. Yet his own research uses variables (e.g. grade averages) that are just as broad as traditional measures (such as IQ) and does not translate his theory into a practical pedagogical model for pre-empting or remedying individual pupils' errors in relation to remedial education, which inevitably deals with cases in which failure to learn has reinforced itself throughout the pupil's career.

Nor is it easy to recognize in Bloom's discussion the realities of schools and classrooms. His concern is with the formal cognitive curriculum, with affect appearing only as a precondition, an influence, or a side-effect. He implies that the achievement of cognitive learning is the main goal of classroom endeavour for teacher and pupil. But classroom motives are not that simple, or aspirations that high. For many pupils the main goal is to get through one's work without 'getting stuck', and to avoid getting into trouble. For teachers, a lesson may be judged successful because the pupils are 'involved', because one has done a satisfying piece of teaching, or because each pupil receives some individual attention.

More generally, Bloom's utopian vision conflicts with other beliefs about social and educational justice: for example, that we should show the less able pupils that we accept them as people (and not make unnatural demands on them for attainment); that mastery learning is disproportionately concerned with those who have difficulties, and *therefore* the more able must be achieving less than they might. These are not just excuses for not trying harder. These views are expressed by caring teachers, and they touch on fundamental tensions within comprehensive education.

Optimism at the Chalk-face

Nevertheless we have found no reason to doubt Bloom's central premise: that usable explanations of success and failure on particular learning tasks are to be found in the classroom, that such successes and failures are cumulative, and that the idea of 'general ability' is unnecessary and unhelpful.

It has been abundantly clear that mastery learning is not achieved simply by providing materials for use in teaching or testing. Teachers can readily develop limited versions of core and extensions or of criterion-referenced assessment and use these so that little change occurs in the classroom (Drever, 1982). But whenever we could induce teachers to suspend belief in 'general ability' and act instead on Bloom's hypothesis, then we found that they began to look critically at curriculum and assessment and to experiment creatively in their classrooms; and they reported an improvement in pupils' motivation and performance. This may of course have resulted mainly from their enthusiasm in trying out something new of their own devising. But the boost to their morale was real enough, and that could lead into further cycles of action and reflection.

Mastery Learning and School Decision-making

Even the few examples quoted show that Bloom's ideas have widespread implications for school policy. But school policy making cannot guarantee that *ideas* thrive. One reason is that the many diverse and conflicting demands on schools lead to a style of instant decision making at every level that deals only with what can be disposed of quickly. In a one-period meeting, mastery learning may be dealt with only as petty administration and short-term contingencies. Discussion of the ideas and major issues will be postponed or glossed over.

Also, while staff accept that there should be a uniform policy on important matters, heads of departments skilfully argue for 'flexibility' because of the distinctive needs of their subject, and teachers similarly ensure that departmental policies allow room for them to teach in their own ways. This prevents confrontations but allows people to avoid the challenge of new ideas.

It is not that teachers *cannot* discuss ideas. The implications of Bloom's theory were extensively debated at meetings of the teachers' steering committee, and again when we brought departmental staffs to the university for a day. But then they were free to organize their own discussions and under no pressure to make quick decisions. The currently fashionable intensive in-service workshops which must produce something useful, would simply have recreated school conditions. Teachers need time, to *think*.

A Mastery Approach to Innovation?

'Traditional' teaching proceeded as if all pupils had the prerequisites for their task, and never explored what these might be. Curriculum developers often treat teachers in the same way, and with the same results.

Teachers are increasingly being asked to accept a fuller responsibility, of *creating conditions conducive to pupils' learning,* and mastery learning offers exciting possibilities of doing so. Should not curriculum developers then apply the same approach, by finding out what skills, knowledge, understanding and motivations teachers have that are relevant to their new task; by providing feedback, reinforcement and sufficient time-on-task; and above all, by accepting that it is not useful to blame failure on teachers' 'lack of ability'?

Our research suggests that this is necessary, and we hope now to develop a fuller exposition of Bloom's theory, that takes account of the conditions affecting teaching as well as those affecting learning. Our main fear is that because Munn failed to regenerate our ideology of 'ability', Bloom will be used to claim that 'teachers are to blame if pupils fail to learn efficiently what their ability entitles them to learn'. That would give us the worst of both worlds.

References

BLOOM, B.S. (1976). *Human Characteristics and School Learning.* New York: McGraw-Hill.

BLOOM, B.S. (1979). *Alterable Variables: the New Direction in Educational Research.* Edinburgh: The Scottish Council for Research in Education.

DREVER, E.L. (1982). 'Curriculum Objectives as Assessment Criteria – Some Problems of Validity', *Programmed Learning and Educational Technology,* 20, 54–57.

SCOTTISH EDUCATION DEPARTMENT (1977). *The Structure of the Curriculum in the Third and Fourth Years of the Scottish Secondary School (The Munn Report).* Edinburgh: HMSO.

SCOTTISH EDUCATION DEPARTMENT (1978). *The Education of Pupils with Learning Difficulties in Primary and Secondary Schools in Scotland.* Edinburgh: HMSO.

CHAPTER 7
Diagnostic Assessment and its Contribution to Pupils' Learning

Mary Simpson

Introduction

The Dunning Report (Scottish Education Department (SED), 1977) viewed diagnostic assessment and assessment for certification purposes as being intrinsically different processes, and stressed the importance of diagnostic assessment for education in its unequivocal assertion that 'it is insufficient to devise curricular objectives and to find out whether they have been attained by each pupil; for those who are not successful the reasons for misunderstandings require to be identified and alternative methods adopted.' In this chapter I shall argue that pupil learning difficulties are commonly the result of unrecognized inadequacies in instructional strategies and practices, that these can indeed be identified by diagnostic testing and that significant advances in educational practice are likely to be critically dependent on the use in schools of genuinely diagnostic assessment procedures. Many of these ideas were developed in the course of studies of the difficulties encountered by 'O' grade pupils in understanding particular topics in biology. The discovery of serious learning problems among pupils who are not normlly regarded as requiring remedial attention suggests that they are likely to be even more widespread and intense among the slower learners who nowadays would be selected for courses at less demanding levels of certification. Although the studies were confined to biology, they have their counterparts in other science subjects and I consider their conclusions to be generalizable across much of the curriculum.

In education, a pervasive myth is that pupil attainment is only to a limited extent affected by changes in teaching strategies and is almost wholly determined by factors which are intrinsic to the pupils: their intelligence, application and motivation. The power of this myth is shown by the extent to which major educational innovations are reinterpreted in terms of its 'explanatory' framework. There are now clear signs that the concept of diagnostic assessment is being revised in this way. Thus, many of the 'diagnostic' tests which have been produced following publication of the report, consist of no more than assessments referenced to course objectives. As such, they serve to identify the topic areas in which learning failure may have occurred but do not illuminate the reasons underlying failure. Their limitations as diagnostic instruments are revealed by the forms of remediation to which they point. Advice is directed towards the pupil and is of the form 'you should revise', 'read your book at home more often', 'do the remedial worksheets', the latter amounting to little more than a different presentation of substantially similar course material. Any claim that tests referenced to course objectives are inherently diagnostic rests on the assumptions that learning difficulties are defined by the topic area in which they occur and they only arise from the pupils' own deficiencies (Simpson and Arnold, 1983). I shall argue that neither of these assumptions is valid and shall reserve the term diagnostic for those activities designed to discover the underlying reasons for pupil failure.

The view that it is deficiencies in the pupil which set the current limits to learning and are responsible for failure would be difficult to sustain if it were shown that under different conditions of instruction pupils learn much more than they presently do, and that traditional teaching practices create difficulties for all but a minority. Under conditions of conventional classroom instruction, a clear relationship exists between attainment and the personal and social characteristics of the pupil. However, this relationship is not maintained in certain qualitatively different, novel teaching schemes devised to take account of well-established principles of learning. In these, about 80 per cent of pupils attain levels normally reached by only 20 per cent of pupils receiving conventional instruction (Bloom, 1976; Nordin, 1980; Case, 1980; Anania, 1983). Moreover, Johnstone and Kellett (1980, chemistry), Dow *et al.* (1978, physics) and Arnold and Simpson (1980, 1982) and Simpson and Arnold (1982a, 1982b) (biology) have identified serious deficiencies in teaching strategies which clearly contribute to many of the common learning difficulties.

Investigations of Pupil Learning Difficulties

During the last few years our work, based in the biology department at Aberdeen College of Education, has investigated the difficulties encountered by secondary pupils in understanding such topics as photosynthesis, osmosis and digestion. These difficulties were puzzling since they were displayed by even 'O' grade pupils, commonly regarded as comparatively able and motivated, and the topics appeared not to demand unreasonably sophisticated levels of reasoning. Our investigations started with open-ended discussions with individuals or pairs of pupils from which emerged hypotheses about the sources of difficulty. These were then checked by objective tests extended by semi-structured interviews in which pupils amplified and gave reasons for their answers. Our methods were designed to find out not how much the pupils could remember of what they had been taught, but *what they actually knew.* Because we wished to chart the development of the pupils' knowledge and ideas these were assessed among pupils from late primary and the first four years of secondary school (S1 to S4). These diagnostic assessments of pupil learning were paralleled by detailed examinations of the topic content and of the teaching material used in the schools.

In all our studies there was clear evidence that the pupils had resorted to rote learning in an attempt to compensate for failure to gain understanding. Correct answers to familiar questions were abandoned when the context of the question was changed and even those pupils whose scores on the more conventional test items would have been regarded as entirely adequate, showed by their answers to further questions a basic lack of understanding of the topics. Moreover, the answers to questions which examined the pupils' possession of 'wrong' knowledge revealed a widespread acceptance of 'explanations' and 'facts' which were wholly incompatible with the material they had been taught.

Barriers to Learning

In discussions with pupils it became apparent that they valued the 'O' grade certificate and were prepared to work for it, but interest in *understanding* science had been lost by all but a minority. Their concern in tests and in homework was with the overall mark and not in the test items which they had failed and which could have served to pin-point where their understanding was inadequate. Some were clearly bored, particularly with laboratory practicals, others were lost and felt themselves to be stupid; the majority seemed to feel considerable frustration in their attempts to understand much of the material presented. All appeared to regard the subject as a series of disconnected topics and none had perceived its central themes, e.g. energy flow in living systems.

Pupils entered S3 classes with unknown and widely different levels of concept attainment, different misconceptions, different learning strategies and perceptions of which strategies were useful, and with different histories of exposure to the many styles of teaching. They were nevertheless subsequently taught by lock-step procedures as if they were homogeneous groups. Some were clearly not extended and others were left floundering, either because the teacher had not detected their difficulties or had been unable, due to the constraints of time and syllabus, to do more than recommend the usual revision exercises.

Our studies showed that not only were pupils restricted in their learning by the impersonal class-based instruction, but were also obstructed by difficulties arising out of deficiencies in the teaching of the course content. Two sources of learning difficulty which are of critical importance are inadequate concept development and the possession of wrong information.

Inadequate Concept Development

In all our studies we found that pupils who had been taught, and were therefore expected to understand, the mechanisms underlying important but complex biological processes had such a poorly developed understanding of the simpler concepts on which the given explanations were based that comprehension was denied to all but a minority. In order to understand the topics of photosynthesis and respiration at 'O' grade, for example, it was essential that they had gained from earlier courses robust concepts of living things, gases, food and energy. They had not. Pupils at the end of S2 had not significantly developed beyond the Primary 7 level in their ability to classify items as living or non-living; 30 per cent of S4 pupils used words and images to describe a gas which were equivalent to those used by primary pupils; 51 per cent and 35 per cent respectively of S3 pupils were unable to classify correctly as solid, liquid or gas, two materials most pertinent to the photosynthesis story, *viz*. carbon and carbohydrate (Simpson and Arnold, 1982a). Further, in order to make any sense out of the proffered explanations of the mechanisms involved in osmosis, pupils must have accurate concepts of a solution. We found few who had. For example, 44 per cent of the pupils believed that if a solution was allowed to stand, the solute molecules would settle out in the bottom of the container. Our findings confirmed Dow *et al.'s* (1978) report that many learning difficulties encountered in some topics in chemistry and physics are attributable to the pupils' failure to gain the necessary basic concepts of solids, liquids and gases.

It was surprising to find that the teachers who participated in our studies were previously unaware of the extent to which their pupils were ignorant of the basic knowledge of these concepts which were necessary for meaningful learning. A detailed scrutiny of the teaching material of the S1 to S4 courses helped to explain the pupils' ignorance. Despite the concern of the course planners that concept acquisition should be of prime importance in science education (SED, 1969), the teaching material used dealt with a wide range of topics but left pupils to guess at the characteristics of the underlying concepts. Concept recognition and discrimination exercises were conspicuously absent and teachers had neither monitored the acquisition of concepts throughout S1 and S2 nor had checked for their attainment in any effective way on the pupils' entry to S3.

It is to be expected that pupils who have received such inadequate instruction in concepts should develop for themselves faulty rules of classification. Nevertheless we and the teachers were surprised to discover just how widely such faulty rules were to be found (Simpson, 1983). More than 70 per cent of certificate biology pupils thought that a worm, a human being and a tree were not made of atoms and molecules and a similar proportion thought that energy, heat and light were. These pupils appear to have derived, undetected by their teachers, a simple classification rule: 'if it is in biology, it is made of cells; if it is in chemistry and physics, it is atoms and molecules'! This must provide the shakiest of foundations on which to build any further knowledge of science.

Possession of Wrong Information

Pupils learn by a process which involves the interaction of new information with their existing cognitive structures. If what they already know is inaccurate and is not specifically corrected, what they subsequently learn, even from well-presented teaching material, is likely also to be incorrect, or acquired merely by rote. In our studies we found that incorrect ideas were widespread among the pupils. Because these ideas had not been revealed by the usual form of classroom tests, whether norm- or criterion-referenced, many teachers were either unaware of their presence or thought them unimportant and had therefore not attempted any remediation. Two types of wrong information may be distinguished: misconceptions which are errors of fact occurring in relative isolation from other facts; and alternative frameworks (Driver and Easley, 1978), which are more elaborate constructions and explanations developed by the learner in an attempt to make sense of his or her life experiences.

One example of the host of learning difficulties caused by undetected misconceptions is drawn from our study of osmosis. The pupils were taught that 'the smaller water molecules pass through the membrane, while the larger sucrose molecules do not' and were expected to learn that *all* the water molecules, being small, can pass through the semi-permeable membrane, and that *none* of the sucrose molecules, being large, can pass. However, approximately half of the pupils believed that water and sucrose molecules each exist in a variety of sizes. Clearly it was possible for these pupils to deduce, erroneously, that some sucrose molecules are small enough to pass, while some water molecules are large enough to be retained. The resulting confusion of pupils and frustration of teachers could perhaps have been avoided if the latter had been aware of the underlying error.

Science teaching normally involves the presentation of facts and experimental observations, and the use of these to construct the theories which explain and unite them. However, what pupils learn can be unexpectedly different from what is taught (Simpson and Arnold, 1982b). It is not uncommon for pupils to select from the facts offered and to construct from them simpler, more concrete, though less comprehensive theories (alternative frameworks) which are extremely resistant to correction. We found evidence of the presence and influence of alternative frameworks in all the biology topics which we examined. For example, when digestion and respiration were taught, pupils were expected to extend their existing simple knowledge of the breakdown of food, of food as a source of energy and of how food is 'burned up' in the body. In every class we examined we found that many pupils had learned not the intended explanations, but instead that the energy releasing process is digestion (not respiration), it therefore occurs in the stomach (not the cells), breakdown is achieved by the acid (not the enzymes), respiration is about CO_2 release (not energy release) and therefore occurs in the lungs (not the cells). Other alternative frameworks have been identified which interfere with learning in physics (Viennot, 1979; Driver, 1983) and in other topics in biology (Brumby, 1979; Deadman and Kelly, 1978) and will undoubtedly be found elsewhere. Their presence and influence on learning are not revealed by normal classroom tests and they tend not to be detected unless the teacher is actively looking for them.

Diagnosis

In their relationships with adults, children are often treated as merely the passive receivers of adult knowledge rather than as active processors of information and producers of ideas. The more formalized the relationship, the more likely this is to occur. The immediate responses of the teachers to the results of our assessments which showed that pupils had not gained the expected knowledge were ones of disbelief – 'But they should have known that!' When shown that pupils had gained incorrect knowledge, they were indignant – 'But I never taught them *that*!' It was as if their pupils had been expected to learn the greater part of what they had been taught, and to learn *only* what they had been taught. If this model of pupil learning were true then diagnosis of pupil learning difficulties could be restricted to the identification of those items of information which have not been acquired. However, learning in children is not an occasional activity; it is a natural and continuous process, and what they have been taught in school amounts to no more than one input of information among many. The process of making sense of information and of achieving meaningful as opposed to rote learning, is one of establishing relationships between the new experience or information offered and what the pupil already knows. Failure to learn will result if that experience or information is not accurately perceived by the pupil, if the pupil has inadequacies in prerequisite concepts or deficiencies in knowledge which preclude any connection with the new information, or if the pupil possesses knowledge which has incorrect elements, derived from previous experiences, which result in the wrong connections being made. Learning difficulties are thus likely to be highly idiosyncratic.

Diagnosis should, therefore, involve the following questions:

What does the pupil 'know' when a particular wrong answer is given to a test question?

Why does that particular answer make more sense to the pupil than the correct answer?

What does the pupil need to know to answer the question correctly?

Did the learning experience offered in class make it clear to the pupil what was to be learned?

Was the information given unambiguous, were the critical ideas salient, and were there inherent possibilities of confusion?

What did the pupil need to know to understand the taught material?

Was that prior knowledge made available in previous courses?

Some of these questions require of the teachers a critical evaluation of the standard teaching practices of their subject specialty; others require the teacher to consider how and what the pupils learn from those practices. These are difficult and demanding requirements. Many teachers see the constraints under which they teach as tending to make them examine their teaching more in managerial than in educational terms and they clearly valued the contribution of the analytical 'outsider' (the researcher) in helping them to reconsider their teaching strategies in the light of the actual learning outcomes.

Some diagnostic information can undoubtedly be derived from criterion-referenced assessments conventionally used to see whether pupils have gained the right information or objectives. When the purpose is diagnosis, however, it is the wrong or inconsistent answers and the analysis of their characteristics which are important. Our diagnostic investigations were more detailed. They covered not only the topic area but also its prerequisite concepts and examined the same aspects of the topic several times, using test items in which there was a change of context or emphasis, to check the robustness of the pupils' knowledge; they also included items which specifically examined the pupils' possession of wrong information and faulty concepts.

The main difficulty in setting up diagnostic tests of this type lies in discovering the kinds of wrong information and faulty concepts which should be examined. Teachers were not only unaware of the source of their pupils' difficulties but their rating of parts of the topic as 'easy' or 'difficult' occasionally bore little relationship to our actual findings. They were experienced, committed and enthusiastic, but the perceptual framework within which they operated was one in which the course objectives, the right information and well-organized teaching were paramount; they were unaccustomed and were indeed not trained to think of their work in the radically different framework of the cognitive processes which are involved when pupils are trying to learn a specialist subject and of the ways in which learning can go wrong despite the genuine efforts of pupils to learn.

We used semi-structured interviews with open-ended questions to probe the pupils' knowledge and the concepts on which it was based. Since our concern was to discover rather than evaluate what pupils knew, we took particular care to avoid hints to the pupils that their answers were to be judged as right or wrong. These discussions provided much clearer clues to the sources of learning difficulties than were given by class test results or the information supplied by teachers and we were left in no doubt that listening to pupil talk should be regarded as the most important single diagnostic activity of the teacher. It is an illusion to think that pupil learning difficulties can be detected and defined by 'diagnostic tests' alone and it is inevitable that difficulties will continue to remain undiagnosed until listening to pupils plays a much larger role in classroom activities. If listening is to be diagnostic, the teacher must encourage the fullest exposition of the pupil's knowledge, right or wrong, in the pupil's own words. This activity is only possible if teachers are prepared to move away from their secure roles as experts and examiners and towards the less certain role of advisers and learning specialists. Such a form of diagnosis may be difficult to incorporate into classrooms where the 'discussion' between pupils and the teacher is governed by rigid conventions and in which, by tradition, it is the teachers who talk and it is the pupils who listen. Possible procedures for encouraging pupil talk have been described by Francis (1982) and by Hornsey and Horsfield (1982).

The longer that cognitive difficulties remain undiagnosed, the greater will be the damage to learning and the more difficult will be remediation. Diagnosis should therefore be a continuous process. This does not imply that formal diagnostic tests should be continually applied, but rather that the normal classroom teaching should be informed by diagnostic principles. To permit this, there needs to be a deliberate shift of attention from the subject and the course objectives to the learning processes of the pupils.

When tests are applied it is strongly recommended that pupils should mark their own answers and that they should discuss these answers with their teachers (Black and Dockrell, 1980; Arnold and Simpson, 1981).

Since it is important that pupils recognize that diagnostic tests are designed to help rather than judge them, the results of diagnostic tests should not be incorporated into summative assessments and this distinctive function of diagnostic tests should be made clear to pupils.

Remediation and Prevention of Learning Difficulties

Once the source of learning failure has been diagnosed (Simpson and Arnold, 1984), the form of appropriate remediation may become clear: misconceptions may be removed by discussions with the teacher; difficulties arising from inadequacies in earlier courses may be dealt with by, for example, selected concept recognition and discrimination exercises; problems of handling large amounts of information may be eased by showing pupils how these can be classified into smaller more manageable units by 'chunking' (Johnstone and Kellett, 1980). Difficulties arising from the pupils' possession of alternative frameworks however are much more resistant to direct remediation. These explanations are based on erroneous but mutually supportive ideas which have been derived from the pupils' own interpretation of events, are commonly at a lower level of abstraction and therefore simpler and more attractive to the pupil than the prescribed theories, and are commonly reinforced by popular opinion. Their displacement by the approved theories is extremely difficult and seldom occurs merely as a result of the formal presentation of new conflicting information (Driver and Easley, 1978; Brumby, 1979). Nussbaum and Novick (1981) have reported encouraging results from a structured approach in which the pupils explain and explore their own ideas, are confronted with conflicting evidence, discover the inadequacies of their own explanations and are assisted to reinvent or explore for themselves the more powerful, approved theories.

In the long term, it is likely to prove more cost-effective and certainly better for the self-esteem of the pupil to prevent than to remediate pupil learning difficulties. Criterion-referenced assessment, as currently practised, directs attention to curricular goals and to the action to be taken by the pupils for their attainment. The diagnostic approach will direct some of that attention to the learning needs of the pupils and the remediation which it suggests is likely to take the form: 'the teacher should devise teaching strategies which are appropriate to those needs'.

Many learning difficulties could be prevented if certain inadequacies in course content and presentation were to be remedied. Two of the many areas in which improvement is necessary are discussed below.

Concepts are not fixed items of information which can be straightforwardly taught. They are ways of classifying which enable some events and processes to be related to or distinguished from other events and processes; they are constantly developing in the pupils' minds and can go awry unless much greater care is taken than at present. The key concepts which are necessary to the understanding of subject topics in the years S1 to S4 should be identified and a strategy of concept development agreed in the school which will ensure that pupils arrive at the various stages of their courses with appropriate preparation. Much more attention must be paid to their formal teaching, testing and revision and course material must contain identification and discrimination exercises (Markle, 1975; Merrill and Tennyson, 1977; Herron *et al.*, 1977). Ideally, the attainment of these concepts should be made 'intended learning outcomes' as was done by Black and Goring (1983) in geography. At present, the constraints of the syllabus deny the necessary time for adequate instruction in concepts. But if pupils are to understand more than they now do, time must be made available, even though this may have to be at the expense of a contraction of the syllabus.

A second, preventable, cause of learning difficulties results from an inadequate consideration of *why* pupils should be expected to gain particular knowledge at specific stages in their education and of what level of abstraction is appropriate. The present syllabus appears to suggest that most topics, regardless of their complexity should be taught at the explanatory level. This commonly results in the use of teaching strategies which are not matched to the learning needs of pupils (Simpson and Arnold, 1984) and often requires the use of simplifications and 'fictionalizations' which are a source of ambiguity and confusion, and which have to be unlearned at a later stage (Dow *et al.*, 1978; Simpson and Arnold, 1982a, 1982b). Reconsideration might suggest a less stringent requirement, that pupils be able to understand certain topics at the descriptive level and to use their knowledge predictively, i.e. to know that 'X will occur' rather than to know why and how.

Implications

Pupils' learning failures have always been a central preoccupation of teachers and education administrators. But the focus of concern has been the assessment of differences in the incidence of failure among pupils to select them for various types of instruction and to grade them according to levels of attainment for the convenience of employers or of other educationalists.

The Dunning Committee took the wider view of assessment: that it should not merely be concerned with certification, but should make a positive contribution to teaching and learning by identifying the reasons underlying failure and by prescribing remedies. It may appear paradoxical to predict that the net result of a move from 'assessment as sorting' to 'assessment as diagnosis' is likely to be a decrease in the emphasis placed on remediation. This follows because research on pupil learning difficulties seems certain to confirm that many of these may be prevented by changes in teaching practice, so that remediation becomes unnecessary.

Many of the necessary changes outlined in this chapter can be incorporated into current educational procedures; others are more radical. What is required is that educational methods should be developed which take full account of the psychological processes involved when pupils learn. There is now a growing body of evidence which suggests that two of the determinants of Piagetian levels of reasoning, the size of the working memory available for a task and the selection of appropriate information processing strategies, can be improved by particular forms of teaching (see Case, 1980, for a review). These methods have yet to be extended to the teaching of specialist subjects and would undoubtedly be difficult to implement in the context of class instruction. What is certain is that 'individualized learning' and 'resource-based learning' schemes will amount to no more than a repackaging of the old materials and will be equally limited in their effectiveness if they are not informed by more accurate theories of pupil learning.

The myth of pupil deficiencies as the source of learning failure survives because it does not tell people what they do not wish to hear. It absolves teachers and curriculum planners from anything more than token responsibility for pupil learning; it removes the need for administrators to consider the findings of the growing body of educational research which suggests, for example, that the price of an extensive syllabus has been paid at the expense of poorer learning for all, and that all pupils may have the potential to achieve, though at different ages, learning goals which are presently obtained by only a minority.

We should not expect the myth to be exploded by the 'big bang' of the curriculum development which is now in progress; it is more likely to be eroded by the small but steady stream of local innovation resulting from the classroom activities of practising teachers.

References

ANANIA, J. (1983). 'The influence of instructional conditions on student learning and achievement', *Evolution in Education: An International Review Series*, 7, 1, 1–81.

ARNOLD, B. and SIMPSON, M. (1980). *An Investigation of the Development of the Concept Photosynthesis to S.C.E. 'O' Grade*. Aberdeen: Aberdeen College of Education.

ARNOLD, B. and SIMPSON, M. (1981). *Diagnostic Testing for Pupil Difficulties in Osmosis. A Teachers' Handbook*. Aberdeen: Aberdeen College of Education.

ARNOLD, B. and SIMPSON, M. (1982). *Concept Development and Diagnostic Testing – Osmosis in 'O' Grade Biology*. Aberdeen: Aberdeen College of Education.

BLACK, H.D. and DOCKRELL, W.B. (1980). *Diagnostic Assessment: A Teachers' Handbook*. Edinburgh: Scottish Council for Research in Education.

BLACK, H. and GORING, R. (1983). *A Diagnostic Resource in Geography*. Edinburgh: Scottish Council for Research in Education.

BLOOM, B.S. (1976). *Human Characteristics and School Learning*. New York: McGraw-Hill.

BRUMBY, M. (1979). 'Problems in learning the concept of natural selection', *Journal of Biological Education*, 13, 2, 119–122.

CASE, R. (1980). 'Implications of neo-Piagetian theory for improving the design of instruction.' In: KIRBY and BIGGS (1980), *infra*.

DEADMAN, J.A. and KELLY, P.S. (1978). 'What do secondary school boys understand about evolutions and heredity before they are taught the topics?' *Journal of Biological Education*, 12, 1, 7–15.

DOW, W.M., AULD, J. and WILSON, D. (1978). *Pupils' Concepts of Gases, Liquids and Solids*. Dundee: Dundee College of Education.

DRIVER, R. (1983). *The Pupil as Scientist?* Milton Keynes: The Open University Press.

DRIVER, R. and EASLEY, J. (1978). 'Pupils and paradigms: a review of literature related to concept development in adolescent science students', *Studies in Science Education*, 5, 61–84.

FRANCIS, E. (1982). *Learning to Discuss: a Report of the Moray House Discussion Skills Project*. Edinburgh: Moray House College of Education.

HERRON, J.D., CANTU, L.L., WARD, R. and SPRINIVASAN, V. (1977). 'Problems associated with concept analysis', *Science Education*, 61, 2, 185–199.

HORNSEY, M. and HORSFIELD, J. (1982). 'Pupils' discussion in science: a stratagem to enhance quantity and quality', *School Science Review*, 63, 225, 763–767.

JOHNSTONE, A.H. and KELLETT, N.C. (1980). 'Learning difficulties in school science – towards a working hypothesis', *European Journal of Science Education*, 2, 2, 175–181.

KIRBY, J.R. and BIGGS, J.B. (Eds) (1980). *Cognition, Development, and Instruction*. London: Academic Press.

MARKLE, S.M. (1975) 'They teach concepts, don't they?' *Educational Researcher*, 4, 3–9.

MERRILL, M.P. and TENNYSON, R.D. (1977). *Teaching Concepts: An Instructional Design Guide*. Englewood Cliffs, N.J.: Educational Technology Publications.

NORDIN, A.B. (1980). 'Improving learning: An experiment in rural primary schools in Malaysia', *Evolution in Education: An International Review Series*, 4, 2, 143–263.

NUSSBAUM, J. and NOVICK, S. (1981). 'Brainstorming in the classroom to invent a model; a case study', *School Science Review*, 62, 221, 771–778.

SCOTTISH EDUCATION DEPARTMENT (1969). *Curriculum Paper 7: Science for General Education*. Edinburgh: HMSO.

SCOTTISH EDUCATION DEPARTMENT (1977). *Assessment for All: Report of the Committee to Review Assessment in the Third and Fourth Years of Secondary Education in Scotland*. (The Dunning Report). Edinburgh: HMSO.

SIMPSON, M. (1983). 'The molecell rules – O.K.?' *Biology Newsletter*, 42, 7–11. Aberdeen: Aberdeen College of Education.

SIMPSON, M. and ARNOLD, B. (1982a). 'Availability of prerequisite concepts for learning biology at certificate level', *Journal of Biological Education*, 16, 1, 65–72.

SIMPSON, M. and ARNOLD, B. (1982b). 'The inappropriate use of subsumers in biology learning', *European Journal of Science Education*, 4, 2, 173–182.

SIMPSON, M. and ARNOLD, B. (1983). 'Diagnostic tests and criterion-referenced assessments; their contribution to the resolution of pupil learning difficulties', *Programmed Learning and Educational Technology*, 20, 1, 36–42.

SIMPSON, M. and ARNOLD, B. (1984). *Diagnosis in Action*. Occasional Paper No. 1. Aberdeen: Aberdeen College of Education.

VIENNOT, L. (1979). 'Spontaneous reasoning in elementary dynamics', *European Journal of Science Education*, 1, 2, 205–221.

CHAPTER 8
Certification for a New Era: A Move to Criterion-Referencing?

Peter Martin

Introduction

When Munn and Dunning were rescued from oblivion in 1979 (SED, 1979) the beginning of a new era in Scottish education began. As a result, schools are now being forced to make far-reaching changes in curriculum, teaching methods, and assessment.

In assessment, these changes are most clearly exemplified by

1. certification for all pupils;
2. the attempt to use explicit performance criteria;
3. some real reliance upon internal assessment for the certification process;
4. reporting by means of a profile.

The changes in the new Standard Grade Certification procedures (the replacement for the old Scottish 'O' grades) are the visible face of the Munn and Dunning implementation programme; inevitably, though less visibly, the assessments in schools are evolving as they accommodate to the requirements of the new certification. All these changes reflect, to some extent, a number of fundamental concerns that were expressed in the Dunning Report (SED, 1977a). One major concern was to introduce methods of assessment that would motivate rather than demoralize. It was, therefore, considered important that assessments should describe pupils' real learning successes. Related to this was a concern to provide continuous and detailed assessment of pupils' progress so as to help the teaching/learning processes. The Dunning Committee recognized that, as well as helping teachers and pupils, more detailed information about pupils' positive performance in a whole range of areas should be invaluable to all certificate users, particularly parents and potential employers. Furthermore the committee believed that it is teachers who are in the best position to have a complete understanding of their pupils' performance: for all purposes, including certification, teachers' assessment should be treated as essential.

Because of these concerns about the use of assessment, the Dunning Report advocated the use of criterion-referenced assessment, i.e. assessment which leads to descriptions of pupils' knowledge and skills by evaluating their work against explicit criteria of how they perform. However, it was recognized that systematic criterion-referencing would prove problematic and demand changes within the schools which would be complemented and supported by changes in the formal examination system.

Because the Dunning Report had asserted the potential for criterion-referenced assessment, and because the power of the examination (certification) system for 'assessment-driven' developments in curriculum and pedagogy was recognized, the possibility and potential of criterion-referenced certification (CRC) became apparent. However before CRC could be implemented the desirability of criterion-referenced assessment for certification needed to be evaluated, and the feasibility of CRC needed to be trialled. As a result the criterion-referenced certification project was set up.

In practice the development in the educational system had to proceed: there could be no waiting for a research project that conceivably could fail. Grade Related Criteria (GRC), the means by which pupils' performance is assessed and reported, using a seven-point grading scale with academic subjects being divided into four or five 'elements', have, therefore, now been established for use by the teaching profession and by the Scottish Examination Board (SEB). The award which a pupil will receive is determined by the extent to which he or she has achieved these criteria and the criteria are expressed in two forms. First, there are the 'Extended Grade Related Criteria' which provide a fairly detailed description of the attainments against which teachers have to judge their pupils' performances to arrive at a grade for each element. Secondly, there are 'Summary Grade Related Criteria' which offer GRC in a more concise form for the use of pupils, parents and employers. But GRC are a hybrid: although they do have some of the characteristics of criterion-referencing, they clearly retain important characteristics of norm-referenced assessment, i.e. the traditional kind of assessment that merely distinguishes, by grading, the more able from the less able without describing any individual's ability by reference to what he or she can do.

The Criterion-Referenced Certification Project and its Tentative Scheme for Certification

The Key Elements in the Project Rationale

Our remit was to investigate whether it was possible and desirable to adopt for certification a system of assessment that is criterion-referenced.

Initially the project was to consider the certification of Foundation courses (the least prestigious of the three levels of certification). However, in developing our work, we have kept in mind the successively more demanding General and Credit courses.

We have worked on the principle that the internal assessment which is necessary as part of the certification process, should not be different from the on-going formative assessment of pupils. The main justification of this takes us back to the Dunning Report which was less concerned with certification than with assessment. In it, the formative assessment that is carried out internally within schools is emphasized as being of critical importance for all children. For many it is of greater importance than certification. Hence we determined to focus on internal rather than external assessment. Our whole approach to assessment has been based on the detailed investigation of pupils' performance. Thus in our scrutiny of subjects, we have analysed syllabuses without concern to minimize the number of distinctive components that are identified and have attempted to structure the detail into relatively homogeneous domains according to the structure of the subject-matter. In this our approach differs from that of the national Joint Working Parties (JWP) of the Consultative Committee on the Curriculum (CCC) and the Scottish Examination Board (SEB) who have prepared the 'Guidelines' in each subject: for them the constraint of reporting on a certificate has meant that no more than about five 'elements' for each subject were identified (although for each of these many separate objectives are described).

Our hope that formative and continuous assessment can be used as the basis for certification would be quite unrealistic but for two things. First, the SEB has always claimed that its function is to measure achievement and this is precisely what the criterion-referenced certification project has been concerned to do. Secondly, a purpose requiring less detailed information (in this case certification) can be served by information of the same kind acquired for a more demanding and comprehensive approach (in this case formative assessment).

We have not wanted to decontextualize tasks just so that the assessments can be simplified. In mathematics, which is to be characterized in schools by the use of 'problem solving' activities, it would be simple to make up tests that only examined aspects of 'data processing' such as ability to add, divide, etc. However if certificate examining decontextualizes separate skills in mathematics, then it seems likely that teachers in school will prepare their pupils for their examinations by teaching that eliminates all but a single skill, and we will risk regressing into all that was worst in 'traditional' mathematics teaching. Another facet of our wish not to decontextualize, but to use whole tasks, is that it may sometimes be possible to assess a number of different things in a pupil's performance on a single task. A major concern here is for the 'backwash' effect of the assessment on the teaching, to ensure rather than to deny the meaningful stimulating syllabuses that both the Munn and Dunning Reports have identified as essential.

Implicit in much of our reasoning is the desire to devise assessment that can be used in the classroom as well as in the examination room. This is evident in our concern to develop criteria that can be used flexibly in a variety of contexts. A corollary of this is that we have not centered our work on the production of test material that can be provided as a resource to schools. Such provision might be appropriate for limited areas of the curriculum but could not encompass the whole of it. Furthermore if this approach were adopted in our work it would necessitate the production of test materials, in each subject, to cover all significant components of all the syllabuses in all schools. Failing this there could be a constricting effect on the work of schools. We note however that 'packages' of test materials can play an important part within a more broadly conceptualized CRC framework, e.g. the TAPS Package (Bryce *et al.*, 1983).

A further justification of our approach may be made. It is that schools can be seen as the test bed for the evaluation of techniques and criteria that might be used by the SEB. This derives from the fact that more can be assessed internally than externally, that much assessment can only be done validly within schools (e.g. Talk in English, Practical Skills in Science) and that, consequently, more assessment techniques are feasible with internal assessment.

Our whole strategy embodies a move away from the psychometric approach that has dominated assessment for more than half a century. Our criteria of what constitutes good assessment are more educational and less statistical than in the past. The danger is that we throw out the baby with the bath water. Concepts like objectivity, reliability and validity are still critically important and we seek these characteristics in what we do.

Our project is a research project: all the beliefs that are incorporated in our rationale and that are based on our view of current educational priorities must be put to the test. It is our hypothesis that they will prove feasible and of value to the teaching profession and to the SEB, but the hypothesis still has to be confirmed.

How Detailed Criterion-Referencing Contrasts with SEB Marking Techniques

There exists a tension between diagnostic assessment and certification, which the marking methods used by teachers and the SEB reflects. Thus diagnostic assessment is not practical without detailed criterion-referenced assessment, whereas 'Direct Grading', using Grade Related Criteria, and 'Traditional Marking' are the methods deemed appropriate for certification. Table 1 attempts to tabulate some of the characteristics of these marking methods and to evaluate them for formative and certification purposes.

There are some points in Table 1 that need highlighting.

Traditional marking is of little diagnostic value in schools, because marks fail to reveal exactly what has been learned, what has not and where one skill may have compensated for the lack of another. It is clearly not criterion-referenced. On a scale of marks, cut-off points can be used to define a series of bands/grades and this will be done in some elements of external examinations. The cut-off points will be derived somehow from GRC. However, as the GRC were not designed to evaluate scores, the procedures needed to do so will be complex and subjective and will risk low validity. Traditional marking seems quite inappropriate for continuous formative assessment; it also will be almost impossible for schools to use – except in a norm-referenced way – for estimating pupils' certificate grades.

Direct grading enables GRC to be used. The extended GRC can provide some descriptions of particular knowledge and/or skills but they are, in effect, a long checklist whose components have not been structured so as to provide the most meaningful descriptions. The reporting of assessments based on GRC is by means of 'grade-points': extended GRC do not build up a vignette of a pupil's performance in the way that is possible with a well-structured criterion-referenced system. The critical problem with direct grading using GRC is that, if many separate pieces of work are graded, then for each there will be a grade-point. But since estimates and certificates simply use one grade for each of the five (or so) elements, how are the many assessments within an element to be combined? There is currently no clear answer: the use of GRC is bedevilled by the lack of explicit aggregation rules and the virtual impossibility of developing them.

Detailed criterion-referenced assessment has the potential to serve the certification process, but as yet it could not be applied. Again the aggregation problem still has to be resolved. Aggregation with detailed criterion-referencing does not need to lead to grades; but the wealth of detail accumulated does need to be reduced to make it more intelligible to certificate readers. Because criterion-referenced assessment requires carefully worked out syllabus structures, the development of systematic rules for aggregation should be simpler with it than with extended GRC.

Table 1
The characteristics of marking procedures to be used by the SEB and advocated for CRC

Detailed Criterion-Referenced Assessment	*Direct Grading*	*Traditional Marking*
Criterion-Referenced Assessment	Grade Related Criteria	Norm-Referenced Assessment
Detailed descriptions.	Some description	No description of abilities.
Applied to single pieces of work/items/questions.	Applied to single pieces of work/items/questions.	Applied to whole exam papers or sections of papers.
Can be reported in prose	Reported using grade-points.	Initially simply a score/mark.
Many aspects for each subject which can be classified into sub-domains.	Many separate extended GRC/aspects within about 5 elements per subject.	Assumes a single ability for each score.
Aggregation by explicit systematic rules is, in theory, possible; but in practice much still needs to be done. Succinct report is potentially feasible.	For reporting by summary GRC a hidden aggregation occurs. Rules are not explicit.	Scores can be converted to grades by intuitive application of GRC.
Reliability and validity still not proven.	Potentially unreliable.	Potentially invalid.
Excellent for diagnostic/formative assessment.	Of some (? limited) diagnostic value.	Almost valueless diagnostically.
Good potential for use for production of 'evidence' for SEB.	Satisfactory for production of 'evidence' for SEB.	Questionable value for production of 'evidence'.
Potential for external examinations.	Usable with external examinations.	Easy to use with external examinations.

The basis for Standard Grade Certification

Examples of CRC Assessment

We can illustrate the approach to assessment and aggregation adopted on the criterion-referenced certification project. In mathematics where 'problem solving' is the integrating theme, we have carried out an analysis of problem solving (Martin, 1985) distinguishing four main stages: determination of strategy, identification of appropriate data, application of the mathematical procedures and communication of the results. These subdivide to give nine different stages within problem solving, and hence that number of contexts in which mathematical concepts, relationships and processes have to be applied. A full analysis of the subject demands listing of all the concepts (e.g. pure number, area, rate), relationships (e.g. identity, equality) and processes (e.g. ranking, subtraction) for all the stages and for all the problem contexts used. This listing, which is substantial for even the Foundation course, is structured by taking into account the stage in problem solving, and by classifying together those items that are alike so that there emerges a number of 'domains' that are relatively homogeneous.

Criteria are necessary for all aspects in each domain. For many of them, a simple mastery/non-mastery distinction is all that is needed. Thus in measuring of the length of an object, pupils are either accurate (within prescribed limits) or they are not. Similarly when doing multiplication, they are correct or they are not. However, if the object being measured is exactly an integral number of units long, it is an easier task to measure than if it is an inexact length. This fact has led us to consider the use of criteria in which several levels of performance can be distinguished – though the different levels are no more than the result of the tasks being more or less complex. (Note that different levels do not match GRC grades.) English may be unlike mathematics in that the quality of performance may be genuinely variable and criteria of differing severity can be applied.

Aggregation has been trialled in English, in an exercise in which a Foundation writing paper was re-marked using our system. The task in the trial was to decide which pupils achieved, for writing only, a Foundation Pass (as it was then described: i.e. grade-point 6 now). In our CRC system for assessing writing, there are 27 aspects of writing which could be used in assessing the compositions (Gordon, 1984). Each aspect was fully described and criteria for each were fully documented and explained at an examiner's meeting. The compositions were marked using all of the criteria, and for each one the information available had to be aggregated to obtain the simple decision of pass or fail.

The aspects were categorized as either 'critical', implying that their criteria had to be satisfied; or 'desirable', in which case a certain number were required although no one was essential; or 'unnecessary' in which case they were irrelevant for the kind of writing being undertaken, or only applicable at higher levels of performance. The categorization was based on a consensus of the views of English teachers. Among the critical aspects were some that described the basic skills, such as spelling, that does not impede comprehension. Also critical were aspects such as 'making use of a range of expression' which do more than consider the surface features of writing. Of the desirable aspects pupils had to satisfy at least one of five which are concerned with 'ability to interest the reader'. None of these criteria was 'critical' because pupils have freedom to choose the manner by which they gain the interest of their readers.

Despite the fact that the categorization could be refined and that the whole exercise was relatively time-consuming, the process of aggregation proved successful and could provide a model for use by the SEB.

Conditions Necessary for CRC to Succeed

If CRC (as we conceive it) is to be implemented, certain conditions will need to be met. It will be necessary that: schools make clear decisions to embrace criterion-referencing; teachers share the Dunning Committee's concerns for improving pupil motivation and performance and teaching effectiveness through the use of criterion-referenced assessments; and departments scrutinize what is being taught to identify which skills can be assessed at which stages and develop sound procedures for carrying out their assessment programmes. 'User-friendly' departmental recording procedures will need to be available (or developed), and used. An important aspect of a whole-school policy favouring criterion-referencing will be the systematic and thorough monitoring of the use of assessment so that the school will be able to furnish proof of the authenticity of the information being accumulated.

The endorsement by the SED and the SEB of the use of criterion-referenced assessment for certification will be necessary, as will the use of the same model of criterion-referenced assessment by the SEB and the schools. The use of continuous criterion-referenced assessment in the preparation of school estimates of pupils' attainments in national examinations, and when presenting evidence in the case of appeals against the final grades awarded to pupils, should be actively encouraged. For this there would have to be detailed guidance regarding what assessments were deemed legitimate and what aggregation rules could be used. These guidelines and rules would apply equally to the external examinations set by the SEB and to the internal examinations of schools.

Furthermore, those 'at the chalk face' will need support. For every subject a detailed analysis of fundamental skills or aspects will be needed. To match each of the skills/aspects that are identified, performance criteria and/or test materials will have to be available; and acceptable rules for aggregating all the evidence over the two-year course will need to be provided. As the work of the JWP's was not undertaken with such a criterion-referenced assessment model in mind, the published guidelines do not provide the support required for criterion-referenced certification. The SEB's subject panels, who might seem ideally placed to provide this support, do not have the resources and the time to do so. However research projects such as the CRC project and many of the others in the research programme have been doing this kind of detailed analysis and developing appropriate test and aggregation procedures. It may, therefore, be that the support for a criterion-referenced system will come from those working on research projects.

It should also be noted that considerable in-service education will be essential to support CRC if it is to be used effectively for the good of the pupils in the schools. For this the education authorities and the colleges will need to be heavily involved.

Two Critical Issues

There are two issues that will affect how a criterion-referenced system of certification could eventually be implemented.

The first is the extent to which internal assessment will, in the future, be acceptable for certification above Foundation level. The current situation in which the Secretary of State has decreed that internal assessment is only legitimate in certain exceptional circumstances, at General and Credit levels, is inimical to fully developed CRC. However there has already been some shift from this rigid position. Most significant is the use that may be made of 'internal estimates'. These are made by schools on the basis of their knowledge 'gathered through internal assessment' of those pupils deemed likely to achieve the higher levels of award. Although the internal assessments will not be a part of certification, in cases where there is a 'marked discrepancy' between an internal estimate and the external grade the external examination will be reassessed. We hope that a further shift will occur.

There is a second question that is a serious and urgent one if a multi-function system of assessment is to be introduced. It is, 'How much flexibility can schools have to develop their system to their own specification?' In so far as it is concerned with certification there is a need for some measure of uniformity in the headings for reporting, in what is assessed, and in the standards employed. If it were possible to implement a model of CRC with certification making some use of internal assessment, then could it be possible for schools to define their main skills/aspects themselves, providing always that information based on them could be aggregated to the broader headings in some suitable way? Could we go further so that the criteria are also defined by schools, since this is implicit if there is a choice of aspects?

There is a tension between the standardization required by examination boards with fixed-format certificates and freedom that the schools have been enjoined to exploit. Our question ultimately is, 'Whose system is CRC?'

Our Hopes and Fears for the Future

Causes for Our Hope

There is a recognition by many within the teaching profession that radical changes must be made. The focus on the certification process on Grade-Related Criteria has meant that if there is to be criterion-referenced formative assessment in schools, as Dunning advocated, then schools will have to operate two systems of assessment which are not fully compatible. Yet teachers are genuinely concerned that there should be a diagnostic use of assessment. Our hope derives from the fact that what we are attempting to do, in producing one system of assessment which serves diagnosis as effectively as certification, has been well received.

Our project is concerned with certification and in its continuing work it is being actively supported by the SEB with whom strong links are being established. It is unrealistic, however, to think that the kind of system we envisage could suddenly be adopted. Instead, we consider that changes could be effected by the planned evolution of the SEB's examination procedures and requirements. Of greatest importance would be some set of procedures that would enable teachers to use internal assessments in the preparation of estimates and evidence for the SEB. If validated for this purpose by the SEB, they might initially be offered as an alternative to the present intuitive approaches where teachers base their estimates on the use of Grade Related Criteria. In the longer run we would hope to see the SEB modify its own procedures: making its own criteria more rigorous, the whole examination system more explicit, and starting a phased elimination of traditional marking. In parallel with this, there might be consideration of a more detailed profile using a greater number of headings.

Every Silver Lining Has its Cloud: Our Fears

I have expressed my hopes. But we are not quite into a new era. The transformation of the educational system that began in 1979 will not be complete until the end of the present decade, by which time Munn syllabuses and Dunning examinations will have been applied to all subjects and criterion-referenced certification could have demonstrated its worth. Yet I am fearful about how genuine and how permanent the present changes in the system will be. And as these are less radical than CRC I am more fearful for CRC, since future developments may be blighted if the present changes are not wholly successful.

The implementation of any criterion-referenced methodology on a national scale is problematic. With GRC, teachers may find it possible, quick and convenient to assess pieces of pupil's work by giving the 'right' grade-points without reference to any explicit criteria. GRC may possibly not be robust enough even for their present job far less for providing the springboard into a full-blooded criterion-referenced system.

One way of conceptualizing the current developments is as a half-way stage to the ideals outlined in the Munn and Dunning Reports. Will the educational system move on from this point or slide back? The possibility most teachers hope for is that, once the present developments are over, the whole education system will settle down. But I fear that it may be in a state of unstable equilibrium and, even more, that a semblance of new stability may mask a return to the old ways.

I worry lest the profile, which will make use of about five elements for reporting each subject, will prove unacceptable. The elements may not report those skills that certificate users feel they need for their purposes and overlap between subjects could prove confusing. In addition, with so few elements, there could be uncontrolled aggregation and so much loss of information that the profile will be unhelpful and invalid.

The burden on Scottish teachers, at the present time, is high. Subversion may not be the intention but expediency may force (in)activities that prevent radical changes from occurring. Schools complain that adopting a thorough criterion-referenced system is expensive in terms of staff time and resources. Furthermore, departmental policies to integrate curriculum, assessment and teaching are only practical where time can be made available for departmental planning. Many departments will decide not to use their limited time for this purpose. Our proposals for (i) restricting assessment through careful planning and prioritizing to obtain only essential information, (ii) selecting assessment tasks that can be done quickly and (iii) making use of pupils' self-assessment (Martin, 1984), have not persuaded teachers that in the balance sheet for criterion-referenced assessment the benefits outweigh costs.

The Challenge the Profession Faces

We are confident that criterion-referenced certification could bring about a new era in Scottish education. The current developments take us only part way there. Now the challenge is to the profession. Does it really want the reforms which the Munn and Dunning Committees were set up to effect? Does it want them enough to push on beyond the present intermediate stage? Does it have enough commitment to these reforms to accept that the price paid for systematic criterion-referenced assessment, will, in the short term be high? Does it dare to allow these reforms to be engineered through a change in the SEB's functioning and requirements? Does it dare to believe that criterion-referenced certification might effect a beneficial revolution in Scottish education?

Will the new era really dawn?

References

BRYCE, T., MCCALL, G.K., MACGREGOR, J., ROBERTSON, I.J. and WESTON, R.A.J. (1983). Teacher's Guide in *TAPS Assessment Pack*. London: Heinemann Educational Books.

GORDON, P. (1984). 'The criterion-referenced assessment of English: the CRC approach', *Teaching English*, 17, 3, 18–25.

MCCALL, J. (Ed)(1984). *The Construction and Processing of Criterion-Referenced Assessment*. Papers presented at a National Course, Jordanhill College, Glasgow.

MARTIN, PETER J. (1984). 'An evaluation of the uses of criterion-referencing'. In: MCCALL (1984), *infra*.

MARTIN, P. (1985). *The Criterion-Referenced Assessment of Mathematics: the CRC Approach*. Dundee: Scottish Curriculum Development Service.

SCOTTISH EDUCATION DEPARTMENT (1977a). *Assessment for All: Report of the Committee to Review Assessment in the Third and Fourth Years of Secondary Education in Scotland*. (The Dunning Report). Edinburgh: HMSO.

SCOTTISH EDUCATION DEPARTMENT (1977b). *The Structure of the Curriculum in the Third and Fourth Years of the Scottish Secondary School*. (The Munn Report). Edinburgh: HMSO.

SCOTTISH EDUCATION DEPARTMENT (1979). *Curriculum and Assessment in the Third and Fourth Years of Secondary Education in Scotland: Proposals for Action*. Edinburgh: HMSO.

HAROLD BRIDGES LIBRARY
S. MARTIN'S COLLEGE
LANCASTER

CHAPTER 9
A School-Based Development Programme?

Donald McIntyre

Introduction

During the last few years the Munn and Dunning development programme has been a major concern of many Scottish secondary school teachers. Anyone visiting schools or meeting teachers regularly can hardly have failed to experience the sense of extra pressure which teachers involved in these developments have felt. Frequently this pressure has been thought of as an additional burden to be carried, but quite often teachers seem to have construed it in more positive terms, as the challenge of a problem-solving task demanding a full use of their professional expertise. Either way, it seems clear that whatever developments occur will have come through substantial efforts made within the schools.

It is the nature of this activity in schools, and the ways in which it has been used, which are the concern of this chapter. To what extent will the new curricula and arrangements reflect decisions made in the schools – decisions informed by teachers' experiences, concerns and judgements? To what extent have teachers' problem-solving activities been used to guide other teachers' attempts to do the same? Or have teachers' efforts been used instead to legitimate centrally planned curricula which schools will be expected to implement?

The Argument for School-Based Development

The distinction made here is between school-based development, where teachers in each school plan, try out, evaluate and perhaps finally adopt innovations, and externally planned development, where outside bodies decide upon the innovations which are desirable and then get the schools to implement what they have planned. Given this distinction, the central argument for school-based curriculum development is a simple one: the alternative policy has been widely tried and has been demonstrably unsuccessful, in Scotland and internationally. School-based development is, quite simply, the only kind of curriculum development which stands a chance of success.

Such crude assertion has to be explained and qualified. Why is it that developments planned by 'expert' outside bodies and disseminated to schools are so consistently unsuccessful? Is this in fact the case? In so far as it is, how much confidence can one have that school-based curriculum development would have more success?

The answers to these questions depend on the centrality of teachers to the work of schools and the distinctive complex nature of the tasks of classroom teaching. On the one hand, teachers have established a generally accepted right to autonomy, and a degree of privacy, in their classrooms, provided they meet certain minimal requirements such as covering specified syllabuses, keeping the noise level down, and not assaulting their pupils. Thus unless teachers are willing and able to introduce innovations planned by others into their classroom teaching, these innovations will not be introduced. Teachers cannot be bypassed, and the naive idea of developing 'teacher proof' curriculum materials should have been abandoned by now.

On the other hand, the nature of classroom teaching has important implications for teachers' professional attitudes and the kind of professional expertise on which they depend. Teachers have to fulfil a variety of roles in their classrooms, under considerable pressure, with little time for reflection, and with uncertainty about what will be interesting to pupils, what they will understand, how they will react to new situations, and mundane things like absences, interruptions, and equipment malfunctions. *Good* teaching therefore, depends upon laying emphasis on planning for the short-term, minimizing uncertainty, keeping things simple and giving priority to 'practical' concerns such as resources, classroom control, and the demands of external examinations. This implies that innovations will be accepted or rejected not on the basis of their long-term educational implications but for their immediate 'practical' benefits and demands. The nature of teachers' work also implies that it can be done well only by those who have acquired a considerable repertoire of ways of acting which are more or less automatically brought into play to cope with those situations for which they have been learned to be appropriate. Innovations will be 'practical' in so far as they do not require change in such repertoires, or, just possibly, if adequate guidance is provided about the new classroom procedures required.

The main problems preventing the adoption of externally planned changes in classroom practice seem to arise from the insufficient account taken of teachers' complex repertoires of classroom routines, and of the difficulty of abandoning or modifying them or developing new ones; the practical benefits to be gained through the adoption of such innovations tend, therefore, to seem slight in comparison to the effort required.

There are, however, two kinds of externally planned innovations which *are* accepted by teachers. First, and most commonly, are changes which teachers are powerless to prevent, such as the introduction of 'mixed-ability' classes or of 'inter-disciplinary' courses following decisions at an administrative level. Implementation of such changes involves doing things for which teachers accept themselves as being accountable, like covering the examination syllabus. A second rarer kind of external innovation accepted by teachers is that which *does* provide clear practical benefits from a teacher's perspective. A good example is the provision of published worksheets for pupils: teachers have found these generally helpful in that they save time and effort in lesson planning.

In so far as such innovations are introduced because of their intrinsic merits, it is necessary to qualify the suggestions that externally planned innovation is generally unsuccessful. But such innovations are frequently intended to promote fundamental changes, and these further changes do not tend to happen when the innovations are introduced in this way. Thus it does *not* happen that mixed ability class teaching typically takes account of the distinctive problems and achievements of individuals; new syllabus content is *not* typically presented or used in different ways from previous syllabuses; and the use of worksheets does *not* imply that pupils are encouraged to exercise a greater independence of judgement. At this more fundamental level, even those externally planned innovations which are adopted tend to be unsuccessful in the effects they have upon the curriculum.

Of course it does not follow that school-based curriculum development is likely to be an effective means of introducing radical innovations. Indeed left to themselves, teachers would probably introduce reforms slowly and minimally in order to cope with the problems they experience. External pressures through national examinations and various types of accountability mechanisms can stimulate school-based developments, but only of a restricted and generally educationally undesirable nature. It would be foolish to claim too much for school-based development. However, thoughtful pressure for change from outside the schools, converted into dialogue with teachers, under conditions where morale is sufficiently high for the teachers to reflect upon their educational aspirations and classroom practices within a framework where school-based developments are encouraged, could offer grounds for confidence about fruitful change. In the meantime, what can be asserted is that unless development *is* school-based, it is most unlikely to be more than superficial.

Characteristics of Educational Planning in Scotland

The tendency for educational planning in Scotland to be much more at a national level than in England has been clear during the last hundred years, since the creation of the Scottish Education Department (SED) and the institution of 'the Highers'. The existence of a single national framework of secondary educational qualifications, and more recently of a single examination board, has strengthened a dominant pattern whereby a single national solution is sought in relation to every educational issue or problem which is seen as important.

Overwhelmingly important in determining which issues matter and which resolutions of them are acceptable is the SED. In recent years the SED's influence on decision making has been exercised not only directly through contacts with schools and teachers but also through two statutory bodies, the Consultative Committee on the Curriculum (CCC) and the Scottish Examinations Board (SEB) and their various sub-committees and working parties. Although always in a minority on such bodies, and frequently present only as non-voting assessors, members of Her Majesty's Inspectorate (HMIs) and other SED officials exert a powerful influence on the decisions. They can do this through the system of patronage which decides membership of these bodies, their key positions as secretaries to the committees, their privileged access to information and their influential contacts, and the greater time which they can spend on the work of the committees than people who have other full-time jobs, and ultimately by being in a position to inform committees of which options might be acceptable to the government and be financially supported.

National working parties tend to have several other significant characteristics in common. Like the Munn and Dunning Committees themselves (Brown, 1978), there is the tendency for membership to consist predominantly of those in, or aspiring towards, administrative rather than classroom teaching roles. A second, no doubt related, tendency is for their reports to focus on administrative issues, and neglect classroom realities and teachers' practical professional concerns. Even those national working parties concerned with development in specific subjects, and with a majority of teachers in their membership, generally fail to reflect the practical perspectives of teachers, with the consequence that their innovative ideas about classroom teaching tend in practice to be rejected (e.g. Brown and McIntyre, 1982).

This centralist approach, however, has not been adopted with equal commitment in relation to all aspects of Scottish schooling. Whereas secondary school pupils who were potential candidates for national certificate examinations have seemed to require national syllabuses, arrangements and methodological prescriptions, for younger pupils and those less academically successful much more freedom has been allowed to schools, with national prescriptions being limited to advice often of a rather general nature.

It is difficult to avoid an interpretation that central control has been exercised over those educational decisions which are seen to be most important. Secondary school teachers have certainly had little doubt as to where their priorities should be directed, since it has been only in relation to 'certificate' courses that there have been external exam results which might significantly affect pupils' futures or teachers' reputations. Thus the low status of non-certificate classes and the autonomy allowed schools in relation to these classes have been closely connected, so that much less constructive use has been made of the autonomy than might otherwise have been the case.

The Munn and Dunning Committees reporting against this background of parallel traditions, reflected in their existence, composition, and primary concerns the dominant tradition of national planning for development. They did, however, have the merit of partially recognizing the weaknesses of both traditions, and they elaborated attractive visions of a possible process of curriculum development in secondary schools. The Dunning Report offered a synthesis of the two traditions with schools having responsibility for part of the syllabus planning and of the assessment of pupils at all levels of achievement, thus increasing school-based planning *and* breaking the relationship between low status and autonomous decision making. The Munn Report emphasized the merits of reflective and long-term planning, corporate decision making between and within departments, and relating subject teaching to broad educational goals as desirable elements of school-based curriculum development. But the reports seemed to take little cognizance of the radical changes which their demands implied for working relationships within schools and for classroom teaching (McIntyre, 1978a). Perhaps the greatest weakness of the two reports was their failure to face up to the enormous gap between their picture of how teachers ought to work, individually and corporately, and the realities of working conditions in schools. Their proposals took no account of the reasons for existing patterns of working nor of the incentives which might lead teachers to transform these patterns in the ways envisaged.

The Development Programme: Some Pre-emptive Decisions

In 1980 the government announced a 'Development Programme' in which what may be viewed as the key passage read as follows:

In any changes which are made it will be essential, however, not to hazard the standards of the national examination system. The Government's determination on this point is reinforced by the lack of consensus which prevails over the benefits to be obtained from the widespread introduction of internal syllabuses and assessment at the upper levels. Accordingly the Government intend that internal syllabuses and assessment shall be confined to the Foundation level except in so far as required for practical aspects of subjects at the other levels (SED, 1980:6).

All developments which have followed have to be understood in the light of this critical decision to reject the Dunning Report's proposal for school-based curriculum development and assessment at all levels. That the proposal was rejected on the grounds that 'the standards of the national examination system' must not be risked carried the implication that academic standards at Foundation level remained relatively unimportant: school-based development was still to be something appropriate only for low status courses.

The government accepted, however, 'the principle that pupils of all levels of ability should have the opportunity of obtaining appropriate levels of award in a national certificate, provided the practicability of this can be established at Foundation level' (SED, 1980:6). Quite how assessment and certification at this level might be less practicable than at other levels remains obscure, but this commitment has certainly meant that a major thrust of the activity since 1980 has been to develop procedures for national certification at Foundation level, including the external moderation of school syllabuses and assessments as well as the preparation of external examinations. Thus while the government were unwilling to loosen the central control over course development and assessment for the more academically successful pupils, they were very ready to increase central control over the work of the less successful; low in status such work undoubtedly is, but the government wanted more control over it.

This extension of central control is described in the SEB document *Framework for Decision*:

From the Brunton Report to the raising of the school leaving age, earlier attempts to prepare courses for pupils left out of the SCE examination system have had little lasting success. The expectation of better results on this occasion stems from thorough preparation and more direct involvement of teaching staff in course design and assessment (SED, 1982:13).

This is a curious reversal. The truth is, of course, that all earlier course planning and assessment for such pupils was totally under the control of teachers within schools, or at least within local authorities; there has always been a 'direct involvement of teaching staff'. What is new is a direct involvement of centralized national planning.

Decision Making within the Development Programme

Given the framework prescribing that development of courses and assessments be school-based only at Foundation level, and within the limits of nationally decided guidelines, what else can be asserted about the school-based nature of these developments?

The pilot studies were undoubtedly successful to the extent that many teachers were stimulated to reflect on their purposes and their teaching methods, and to try out new ideas. Such thinking and innovation, and the self-critical evaluations which some teachers made of their efforts (e.g. McNally, 1983) must surely have enriched the education of the pupils concerned and contributed significantly to the professional growth of the teachers themselves. Yet it is difficult to establish a balanced overall picture either of the incidence and quality of such initiative among teachers or of the use made of these within the wider development. There are several reasons for this.

First, it is, in the spring of 1985, impossible to predict with confidence the nature of the courses, patterns of teaching, assessment arrangements or other outcomes of the developments of the last few years. Yet the very concept of 'development' implies that actions and events are to be understood in terms of their consequences. It may be that activities or initiatives which have seemed to those involved, in schools or elsewhere, to have been of central importance will not turn out to be significant in influencing the outcomes of the operation.

Secondly, such doubts are exacerbated by the discontinuities apparent in the programme. Most strikingly, feasibility studies were initiated in schools to contribute to the developments conceived by one set of national planners in each of several subject areas, but while these studies were in progress new national Joint Working Parties (JWPs) of the CCC and the SEB, were appointed to make their own plans. Similarly, while feasibility studies in some subject areas have focused exclusively on the Foundation level, decisions at a national level mean that these will lead directly into implementation at Foundation *and* General levels.

Thirdly, the quality of the information available about the working of the developments has been very uneven. It would be unwise to generalize from the inevitably unrepresentative reports which one receives from other individuals involved in diverse roles within the programme. Yet the research evidence available is restricted to a small number of case studies.

The SEB's published 'Arrangements' for different courses are generally uninformative about decision-making processes, and the crucial *Framework for Decision* document (SED, 1982) gives the impression of being designed to obscure understanding of the relationship of the school-based pilot studies to national decision making. Forces within the SED vetoed a suggested research programme focusing on the ways in which decisions would be made by the Joint Working Parties.

Finally, despite their limitations the various sources give quite consistent indications that there have been major differences between subject or inter-disciplinary areas in preconceptions about, and processes of, course development. It is apparent that any generalizations seeking to encompass these different areas would be unlikely to be illuminating.

Any picture presented of the process of development must be, therefore, confused, incomplete and diversified. Nonetheless, there are a few questions which seem worth asking. The first such question concerns purposes of the feasibility studies. *Framework for Decision* identifies some very general issues of concern in these studies but what questions the studies were designed to answer, and how the studies were designed to address these questions, is not clear. One set of questions could have been concerned with conditions and support conducive to thorough imaginative school-based course planning and evaluation (indicating how schools could be supported in school-based activities). Another set could have been about the kinds of courses best suited to stimulate pupil motivation and learning while being feasible in practical terms (so that such courses could be planned in other schools). But the main conclusion that 'evidence of the pilot experiments confirms that it would be feasible to proceed with implementation of Foundation courses' (SED, 1982:13) implies that the feasibility studies were conceived primarily as a check on the administrative feasibility of national certification at this level.

It may be more fruitful to ask what conception of course development was implicit in the feasibility studies as experienced by teachers. Some variety in teachers' experiences and reactions is reflected in interim reports by Munn and Morrison (1983a, 1983b, 1984) of their study of collaboration among teachers in the three multi-disciplinary courses. In the Health Studies course, teachers seemed to see the course planning as under the control of people outside the school, with teachers merely elaborating on what they were given. In the words of one teacher,

> Somehow I don't think the course has been generated from the bottom up, it's been, it's gradually filtered from above down (Munn and Morrison, 1984, p.45).

Furthermore, teachers were reluctant to make too much effort themselves until a more stable context had been created at national level. In some respects the experiences of Contemporary Social Studies teachers were similar, but they perceived themselves as engaged in school-based development, since they had the tasks of interpreting very generalized guidelines, developing curriculum materials and trying out new approaches to assessment within a broad course structure with which they were not all happy. The danger of wasting effort by 'getting it wrong' was demotivating, but more generally there was a sense of being exploited, of being asked to do extra work with no adequate incentive.

The Social and Vocational Skills course, however, appears to have been experienced as a school-based development *and* won enthusiastic commitment from many teachers. This course organized frequent meetings among pilot school coordinators and it was at these meetings that the guidelines were planned and revised in the light of the schools' experiences. Not only was there a sense of this new course belonging to the teachers concerned, but there was also a sense, apparently lacking in the other two multi-disciplinary courses, that the course planning was necessarily an *investigative* enterprise in which questions had to be asked and answered. Munn and Morrison suggest that the attachment of an action research project to this course may have helped to generate this kind of thinking.

These summary sketches of teachers' reactions to involvement in three multi-disciplinary courses are based on case studies in small numbers of schools. It is possible that the different reactions described reflect as much the specific teams in these schools as they do the courses in general. For present purposes, however, the significant point is that there should be such a spectrum of perceptions and reactions, course development being seen as (i) not school-based, (ii) school-based but as not under teachers' control and as burdensome, or (iii) school-based, under teachers' control and an opportunity for satisfying and fruitful professional activity.

However, in the long run what matters is not the experiences of teachers on the feasibility studies, but the use which is made of these studies. The JWPs, the first of which were set up in September 1982, were in a position to use such information as feasibility studies generated. These JWPs have wide-ranging remits, concerned with aims, objectives, syllabuses, assessment techniques, moderation and guidance for teachers at all three levels of certification; in effect, overall responsibility for planning the S3 and S4 courses for all pupils has been delegated to them. They are of course directly in line with the dominant Scottish tradition of national working parties which conventionally formulate single orthodox solutions to problems, solutions which are generally implemented at an administrative level and have in the past had little impact in terms of educational practice.

In the absence of any study of the working of the JWPs, we must rely on their own accounts of the use they made of information from the feasibility studies. From the *Arrangements in Science* (SEB, 1984a), for example, there is no explicit mention of the feasibility studies. The English JWP asserts that:

> in both philosophical and practical terms, the Arrangements are greatly influenced by the results of the English Foundation Feasibility Study and by the experience of the teachers and development officers involved in it. What modifications have been necessary reflect the differences in scale and complexity occasioned by national certification of a very wide range of ability at S4 (SEB, 1984b:3).

In what follows there is no specification of particular things learned from the feasibility studies. A great deal of advice is offered in both these subject documents and, although it is made clear that this *is* advice rather than prescription, the conscientious teacher anxious to optimize his or her pupils' chances may be stretched to take account of the implications of the advice, without having time or energy to be imaginative as well. It is not easy to see what these documents have learned from the feasibility studies about how teachers can be supported and encouraged in school-based course developments.

In contrast, the *Arrangements in Social and Vocational Skills* (SEB, 1984c) repeatedly offers instances of practices found to be practicable and appropriate in the feasibility studies, constantly reiterates the importance of schools doing what suits their pupils, teachers and contexts, and gives guidance through offering multiple specific examples. The following, discussing 'co-operative activity' as a 'compulsory pupil experience', is typical:

> The precise form which each experience takes should result from an open-ended process of genuine and purposeful negotiation between teachers and pupils, taking account of the needs, interests and abilities of the pupils and, indeed, of the teachers themselves. However teachers might find further guidance helpful and this is given below in pages 11 to 17. The suggestions are based on work done in pilot schools so their practicality has been demonstrated . . .

and

> . . . These are not intended to be used as models, but are offered to illustrate some of the approaches taken in pilot schools and in the hope that they may give inspiration to other schools planning their own, perhaps very different, activities (SEB, 1984c:3).

Whether such guidelines can effectively encourage and facilitate school-based development remains to be seen, but a thoughtful and impressive effort has been made to do just that. It may be regretted that the same sense of practicality, learning from teachers' own efforts, pupil centredness, and openness to new possibilities could not have informed the guidelines offered for some other subject areas.

Conclusion

In the context of this development programme, there has been much thoughtful, enthusiastic and innovative teaching, and a sharing of many valuable ideas among teachers; but whether adequate use has been made of all this constructive activity must be seriously questioned. The development has been school-based only in so far as teachers have been persuaded to invest extra effort into planning and teaching units for their less successful pupils. Decision making has been overwhelmingly in the hands of HMIs, SEB, and JWPs; and so far as the available evidence shows, the feasibility studies were not carefully enough planned for the effort made at school level to be used efficiently in informing the centralized decision making. The fiction that the development has been school-based, with teachers more involved in course planning than in previous years, disguises the fact that decision making about all the innovative features of the programme (curriculum structure, syllabus content, assessment procedures, moderation arrangements and criteria) has been firmly held at the centre; and areas over which teachers previously exerted autonomous control, low-status though they were, have also now been encroached upon by national decision makers. Finally, it is ironic that the one component of the curriculum in which both the conduct of the pilot study and the national planning of guidelines seem to have been carefully planned to promote future initiative at the school level is a course which had no part in the Munn Committee's proposals.

Given such processes of development, is it possible to predict the likely outcomes? The emphasis which has been placed on administrative arrangements, and previous experience showing how effective national planning can be in these terms, give grounds for confidence that a viable system for allocating certificates to pupils is very likely to emerge. This system is likely to be such that, with experience, teachers will develop patterns of teaching calculated not to take risks with their pupils' chances of 'success'; and a concern for such safety will discourage them from exploring thoughtful innovative approaches like those adopted by some during pilot studies. However, the limited incentive for pupils, and therefore for teachers, of working for success at Foundation level may not be sufficient (as it has been, for example, at 'O' grade) to compensate for the alienating effect of working within an externally imposed system. As a result, the Foundation courses of the future, although more structured and coherent than the non-certificate courses of the past, may not be any more rewarding.

References

BROWN, S. (1978). 'The politics of educational reform' In: MCINTYRE, D. (1978b), *infra.*

BROWN, S. and MCINTYRE, D. (1982) 'Costs and rewards of innovation: taking account of the teachers' viewpoint.' In: OLSON, J. (1982), *infra.*

MCINTYRE, D. (1978a). 'The teacher's work and its organisational context'. In: MCINTYRE, D. (1978b), *infra.*

MCINTYRE, D. (Ed)(1978b). *A Critique of the Munn and Dunning Reports.* Stirling Educational Monograph No. 4. Stirling: University of Stirling Department of Education.

MCNALLY, J. (1983). *A Teacher's Analysis of Classroom Talk during a Science Investigation.* Unpublished M.Ed. Dissertation, University of Stirling.

MUNN, P. and MORRISON, A. (1983a). *Contemporary Social Studies Collaboration: The Experience of Two Pilot Schools.* Stirling: University of Stirling Department of Education (mimeo).

MUNN, P. and MORRISON, A. (1983b). *Social and Vocational Skills Collaboration: The Experience of Three Pilot Schools.* Stirling: University of Stirling Department of Education (mimeo).

MUNN, P. and MORRISON, A. (1984). *Health Studies Collaboration: Follow Up Report: Four Pilot Schools.* Stirling: University of Stirling Department of Education (mimeo)

OLSON, J. (Ed)(1982). *Innovation in the Science Curriculum.* London: Croom Helm.

SCOTTISH EXAMINATIONS BOARD (1984a). *Scottish Certificate of Education Standard Grade: Arrangements in Science at Foundation and General Levels.* Dalkeith: SEB (mimeo).

SCOTTISH EXAMINATIONS BOARD (1984b). *Scottish Certificate of Education Standard Grade: Arrangements in English at Foundation, General and Credit Levels.* Dalkeith: SEB (mimeo).

SCOTTISH EXAMINATIONS BOARD (1984c). *Scottish Certificate of Education Standard Grade: Arrangements in Social and Vocational Skills at Foundation and General Levels.* Dalkeith: SEB (mimeo).

SCOTTISH EDUCATION DEPARTMENT (1980). *The Munn and Dunning Reports: The Government's Development Programme.* Edinburgh: SED (mimeo).

SCOTTISH EDUCATION DEPARTMENT (1982). *The Munn and Dunning Reports: Framework for Decision.* Edinburgh: SED (mimeo).

CHAPTER 10
The Role of Research in the Development Programme

Sally Brown

Introduction

The Scottish Education Department (SED) responded to the Munn and Dunning Reports (SED, 1977a and 1977b) by embarking on a development programme (SED, 1980 and 1982). This initiative explored the feasibility of the recommended changes in the curriculum and assessment of pupils during their last two years of compulsory education. Unusually, a research programme was set up as part of the development and 27 projects were commissioned in nine institutions at a cost of about £1 million.

But what, one may ask, was the function of research in a development programme of this kind? What kinds of projects did it commission? What relationship did the research have to the concurrent curriculum developments and decision making? What efforts were made to ensure the research findings and products reached those who could use them?

Responsibilities of the Research Programme

Research within a development of this kind was clearly policy related and expected to address those issues which the Munn and Dunning Reports recommended be investigated. Those recommendations concerned the education of 14- to 16-year-olds but drew distinctions among levels of achievement and curricular demand by the labels 'Foundation', 'General' and 'Credit'. Much of the research mirrored the emphasis which the reports put on innovations in curriculum, assessment or resources for those pupils who achieve at the lowest (Foundation) level, and almost all the projects had close relationships with other developments in the programme. Many were themselves developmental and designed to support teachers implementing the innovations.

A policy-related research programme, however, should not be merely *policy-directed* and support developments derived from that policy. It should also be *policy-informing* and, therefore, inquire into the implications of carrying the policy through to its limits and include projects carried out in wider contexts. It was for this reason that the investigations of the value of innovations like systematic diagnostic assessment, mastery learning strategies or school policies for assessment using criterion-referenced profiles, were designed to work with ages 12 to 14 rather than 14 to 16 on the assumption that pupils must be socialized into the new systems at the *start* of secondary school if they are to reap the potential benefits. Similarly, a research approach to multi-disciplinary developments deliberately worked beyond the boundaries of the SED's 'mainline' developments. It aimed to generate a fuller understanding of this area of innovation, unfamiliar in Scotland, than would be possible if it had, for example, followed the SED's lead in initially designating specific subjects as contributors to these developments.

Their close relationship to the 14 to 16 programme gave the 27 projects a distinctly 'development-specific' characteristic. They were, however, also part of the SED's overall programme of research which shoulders a rather broader educational responsibility. In relation to this responsibility, it was seen as necessary that decisions on whether to fund particular projects would depend on them displaying a potential to extend general knowledge of educational issues regardless of whether the recommendations of Munn and Dunning would eventually be implemented. It was important that, for example, research on writing skills, teachers' management of discussions, assessment in music or collaboration in multi-disciplinary courses, have educational value in a general sense and in the longer term as well as a narrow utility for this particular programme.

This requirement (the essence of coherent research) recognized the main potential of research as offering long-term developments in the general understanding of education, explanations of why things turn out the way they do and ideas which work their 'way into the woodwork of the organisation until the findings are eventually incorporated as part of the overall decision making process' (Leigh, 1980).

In contrast, the more 'development-specific' requirements suggested research should concentrate on solving immediate practical problems and on offering clear-cut indicators for major decisions. The projects frequently found themselves caught up in this tension. On the one hand, they were considered for funding in the first place because of their apparent relevance to difficulties encountered by practitioners. On the other hand, the time taken to set up research and to effect rigorous systematic inquiries militated against the quick resolution of practical problems. Even where research is deliberately associated with development it is still better suited to articulating alternative courses of action or decisions, and elaborating the conditions necessary for and implications of choosing particular alternatives, than to solving the exigencies of teaching.

Before looking at the details of the research projects, there is one area of the 'development-specific' responsibilities which calls for some comment. Any body of innovative ideas, like those of the Munn and Dunning Reports, raises questions about resources. It was tempting to assume that more resources would resolve the practical problems of implementing the innovations. For example, the suggestion that assessment difficulties would disappear if comprehensive banks of test items were developed and categorized for the many purposes which teachers have in assessing pupils in different contexts was seductive. But did research have any role in the provision of such resources? Providing resources was not a responsibility for meagre research budgets but the SED saw a role for research in exploring the *feasibility* of such provision.

In item banking, it was argued, projects in a few schools could, with modest item collections, gather information relevant to important questions like: What investment of money and human resources is required to generate, maintain, use and renew item banks? Under what conditions are teachers willing and able to use such resources? What are the dangers of the technology becoming obsolete or the item collections being unable to respond to changes in the curriculum? What kind of in-service preparation is needed before teachers can take full advantage of the resources?

Responsibilities of this kind for investigating the generation of resources, together with others already mentioned (supporting educational practice in specific areas, providing information relevant to policy decisions and extending general knowledge about education), determined the principles which guided the research programme as a whole. But what particular kinds of research project did the SED choose to support?

The Substance of the Research Programme

The emphasis which the research programme put on assessment was striking. This highlighted the Dunning Committee's enthusiasms for promoting diagnostic assessment as an integral part of teaching (implying strategies like mastery learning), introducing criterion-referenced assessment for reporting as well as diagnostic purposes, formulating individual school policies for assessment, giving schools some responsibility for certification, replacing the Scottish Examination Board (SEB) Ordinary Grade with a three-level Standard Grade for the full range of achievements at 16 and cumulative assessments in the form of pupil profiles for guidance purposes in schools.

The preoccupation of the research with assessment reflected the radical nature of the Dunning Committee's proposals for change from a norm-referenced to a criterion-referenced approach and for schools to accept some responsibility for certification. The curriculum developments' initial school-based model gave responsibility for *course* generation to teachers but encouraged research support on the *assessment* side. This reliance on 'outside experts' reflects a mystique which has traditionally been attached to assessment. The expertise of measurement specialists has baffled the public and led to erroneous assumptions that fundamental changes in assessment cannot be achieved by teachers without sophisticated new techniques and statistics. Furthermore, this mystique has been compounded by the political significance of assessment for teachers. Traditionally they have not given accounts of their 'private' activities in classrooms but accountability has emerged through national certificates and reports to parents and employers. It was hardly surprising, therefore, that teachers did not expect, and were not expected, to undertake either the major developments or the crucial decisions on assessment.

After assessment, the most conspicuous feature of the research was the preponderance of collaborative action research approaches. These were seen as supporting the initial move towards more school-based course construction. Action research involves teachers and researchers collaborating in inquiries; those inquiries are based on practice, test theories grounded in practice and aim both to improve practice and generate knowledge about teaching. The approach calls for a reflective and analytic stance towards teaching and avoids the problems of lack of impact on the classroom and failure to communicate findings to practitioners which are perceived in much conventional research.

As well as reflecting the broad emphases on assessment and action research, the individual projects fell into five categories according to the kind of support they offered the general development programme. In the first category 11 projects, closely associated with schools' course developments, were concerned with conceptualizing and assessing various 'new' skills and competences emerging in those courses. Within this category, however, three distinctive kinds of research aims were to be found.

The first set of aims was concerned with the clarification and assessment of certain skills and competences which (i) occupied central places in the developments, but (ii) carried no guarantees that teachers shared an understanding of their meaning or how they should be assessed. These aims were manifest in research on competence in spoken English, practical skills in science, communicative skills in foreign languages, writing skills among low achievers and some aspects of geography.

A second group of aims was directed towards strategies for teaching and assessment of the various skills and competences. These strategies included mastery learning techniques, 'stations' assessment of practical and communication skills, oral interviews (teacher/pupil), self-assessment, peer-assessment and pair or group tasks.

The third group of aims gave priority to areas of the curriculum which research traditionally has neglected (home economics, physical education, music and business studies) or which were novel in Scottish education (the multi-disciplinary Health Studies course). Action research projects set out to clarify the meaning of 'attainment' in these areas and explore the assessment of various facets of the attainments.

These 11 projects produced exemplar materials, clarifications of skills and competences, assessment techniques and strategies for teaching or assessment. Valuable though this support was for teachers in their creative generation of courses and assessment procedures, it did not offer resources on a large scale. The SED was committed to a second category of projects to explore the feasibility of resource provision. But into what kinds of resources did it put its research investment?

Teachers' preferences were for guidance on assessment or test materials and five projects investigating assessment resources were initiated. One project, on the assessment of reading strategies among low achievers, explored the provision of sets of assessment techniques sufficiently general in nature for teachers to adapt them to their own teaching content. Two other projects, concentrating on mathematics and science at Foundation level, generated item collections classified according to the objectives or other characteristics of the courses. The final two projects developed computer programs for marking pupils' responses to test items, analysing the strengths and weaknesses of their performance (individual or group), selecting items according to teachers' specifications for tests, producing copies of tests and calibrating item difficulties.

The selection of English, mathematics and science as the areas for investigation followed from the SEB's choice of these subjects for their first and longest experiments on school-based developments in the Extended Feasibility Studies (EFS). All five projects accepted responsibility for exploring the possibilities and problems for (i) teachers' use of the resources and (ii) long-term maintenance and renewal of the resources. The orchestration of these concerns was the responsibility of a coordinating committee with representation from each project, SED, SEB and the Convention of Scottish Local Authorities.

Research was by no means exclusively in the English, mathematics and science areas. One group of courses in particular need of research support comprised the multi-disciplinary Contemporary Social Studies (CSS), Health Studies (HS) and Social and Vocational Skills (SVS). These new courses could not assume that they would be seen by teachers as essential or even worthwhile. Without a community of 'multi-disciplinary teachers' and with the SED's stated intention that the courses would be offered at only Foundation and General levels, these developments started with low status, ventured into areas where teachers were inexperienced and depended on collaboration among subjects with disparate values and teaching methods. The unfamiliarity of the courses, however, could be a strength. Teachers had fewer preconceived ideas about what the courses ought to contain, how they might be developed and the ways they should be taught. Multi-disciplinary work offered opportunities for teachers to develop new types of collaboration, new conceptions of knowledge to be acquired by 14- to 16-year-olds, new kinds of courses and new teaching approaches.

With this 'mixed' prognosis, a third category of three projects was designed to foster positive, innovative, multi-disciplinary developments. Among other things, these projects explored the implications of introducing courses which conceived of pupils' learning in two different ways: (i) traditional approaches emphasizing learning *outcomes* (skills, understandings, attitudes) identified by teachers, curriculum developers or learners before the learning takes place, (ii) *process or experiential* approaches emphasizing the learner's own social reconstruction of his or her experiences and with no predetermined outcomes.

One project undertook a curriculum development appropriate for an SVS course which genuinely shunned the specification of content. This research mapped out the tensions experienced when a *process-based* curriculum must operate within a certification system which assesses *products*. A second project, concerned with how 'new' kinds of pupil learning are to be effected in the classroom, aimed to further teachers' understanding of discussion processes and their management of pupils' discussions. The idea that pupils should learn (i) to discuss, and (ii) through discussion, was a salient feature of the multi-disciplinary plans. The third project was directed towards describing the collaboration among teachers when departments had joint responsibility for constructing and teaching courses, and to unravelling the factors influencing that collaboration.

Each of the three project categories above has emphasized research contributions to the thinking and practice of *specific* course developments. Five other projects, however, examined in depth some of the more *general* recommendations of the Munn and Dunning Reports. They constituted a fourth category of fundamental research on 'new ideas' with intentions to clarify and provide a basis of knowledge for future decisions and developments.

Much debate following publication of the reports centred on the 'new ideas' which explicitly or implicitly recommended introducing diagnostic assessment in classrooms, criterion-referenced reports of attainment, mastery learning strategies and the identification of 'target populations' among pupils (all target populations would have certificate awards but these would be discriminated at three levels: Foundation, General and Credit). These ideas were unfamiliar in much of Scottish educational practice, their nature and the implications of their introduction were ill-understood and arguments about their worth were speculative. Research in this category had two main purposes. First, it aimed to illuminate the forms the innovations might take and the conditions necessary for their implementation in schools. Secondly, it provided information relevant to SED/SEB policy decisions by, in particular, investigating (i) the desirability and feasibility of introducing criterion-referenced assessment and certification, and (ii) the help which analyses of existing examinations data could offer in the task of distinguishing between General and Credit performances.

The fifth category was the evaluation programme. The three projects here looked at very different kinds of development. One was a partial evaluation of the EFS in English, mathematics and science, and concentrated on teachers' and pupils' reactions to the early school-based initiatives at Foundation level. The second focused on a centralized local authority exercise directed towards developing secondary school assessment policies and practices. A computer assisted guidance system, relevant to the Dunning Report's recommendation that comprehensive pictures of pupils be assembled for guidance purposes and aiming to provide support for pupils in careers education, was the object of the third evaluation.

The value of evaluation to a wider development programme lies in the increased credibility and understanding it bestows on the developments in the eyes of the public. Given the great range of these developments, the three projects were hardly adequate for the tasks of formative and/or summative evaluation and the fifth category is the major weakness in the structure of the research programme.

The emphases and categories characterizing the research programme identify the *intended* relationships between research and the other developments. In what form did those relationships materialize?

Relationships   Between   Research   and   Concurrent   Curriculum Developments

The curriculum development had two distinctive stages. The school-based EFS in English, mathematics, science and the multi-disciplinary courses were superseded in 1982 by central Joint Working Parties (JWPs) of the SEB and the Consultative Committee on the Curriculum (CCC). These JWPs produced national guidelines for courses and assessment at all levels for the SEB's new Standard Grade award.

During the period of the EFS, all the research projects in relevant subject areas formed links (strongest in science and SVS) with the developments. They visited and provided material for 'pilot' schools and played an active part in EFS conferences. The projects concerned with assessment of practical skills in science and the item banks for Foundation science and mathematics even took some responsibility for national and regional certification trials. In SVS, the 'alternative' research development maintained very close contact with the SED's own development with mutual sharing of ideas, materials and in-service activities.

The effects of these close relationships depended on the influence of the researchers on curriculum decisions. The work on practical skills in science, for example, substantially influenced the final assessment arrangements. Science teachers in the EFS had little experience of practical assessments and were happy to accept a workable scheme prepared by competent researchers. In cognitive areas relevant to item banks, however, teachers were eager to formulate their own course objectives. Researchers would then prepare valid items for these objectives only to find a few weeks later that the objectives had been radically changed. The most 'equal' relationship was established in SVS. The 'alternative' and 'mainline' developments achieved a balance where close cooperation and consultation did not infringe the autonomy of the two complementary development approaches.

The research projects in English followed a more independent path but still had common concerns with the EFS. The inquiries into assessment of reading, writing skills and competence in spoken English reflected three of the four 'modes' around which the EFS was structured. Products of the research, offering conceptual clarifications of and assessment schemes for various aspects of low-achieving pupils' performance in reading, writing and talking, were highly relevant to the development but were not narrowly defined within its boundaries. Two implications arose from this looser research/EFS link: first, although some ideas and preliminary materials were available during the pilot work, the main research products and findings emerged at the end of the EFS; and secondly, those products and findings have substantial value for other age groups (e.g. reading and writing in primary school) and other subjects (e.g. talking across the curriculum).

As the curriculum developments moved on and JWPs were set up consultancy demands on researchers increased. A number of JWPs' reports acknowledged this help from projects and several researchers were JWP members (one a chairman).

The research in home economics, music and physical education was established before the relevant JWPs and in a good position to contribute its recent experiences and findings. In foreign languages and health studies the JWPs and projects emerged at about the same time; with researchers as consultants to the JWPs, a mutual exchange of ideas characterized the development. By the time projects in geography and business studies were commissioned, the JWPs were well underway; the researchers' role, therefore, was not consultancy but collaboration with teachers working with the JWP's reports.

Despite much constructive JWP/research cooperation, there were tensions. The JWPs, with short lives and demanding commitments to make important decisions, often expected research to resolve the immediate, awesome problems facing them. The research, however, was best suited to using its findings from in-depth inquiries to inform decision making in the longer term. Its value should be judged *in the future* by its contributions to those who will (i) up-date the deliberations of the JWPs, or (ii) put the new arrangements into operation. Research support for the latter is evidenced by the extensive involvement of almost 90 per cent of the projects in local authority and national in-service teacher education. Furthermore, although the research programme described here was originally conceived to continue until December 1986 (that is *not* to say that no other research in education 14 to 16 was envisaged beyond that date), by mid-1984 20 projects had produced books, monographs, packages or computer programs concerned with classroom practice and directed towards teachers, students, advisers and HMIs with responsibility for implementing the innovation. Twelve projects had also written books or papers examining the 'big issues' of the proposed changes and of importance to the decision makers and trainers (JWPs, SEB, SED, CCC, colleges and universities and local authorities) as well as the implementers. Since the number of full-time researchers at any one time was little more than a dozen, the projects have made a creditable contribution to the general developments.

Reflections on the Programme

Apart from the relationships between the research projects and the other development initiatives, there were a number of other features of the research programme which might claim to have relevance for the planning of any future policy-related programmes. This final section points to some of those features which I see as particularly important and then offers my views about the lessons to be learned from the programme by researchers and research planners. The features I have chosen to identify are: the pluralistic nature of the research which ensured the strength of the programme, the heightened accountability of researchers arising from their relationships with educational practitioners, the dilemmas to be faced in disseminating the research findings, the opportunities provided by the programme's projects for further research or development, the paucity of independent evaluation studies and the contributions of the research findings to the thinking of educational practitioners and policy makers.

The SED's policy of using the available diversity of expertise and funding researchers with more than 20 different backgrounds (from chemistry to human relations) from nine institutions was a major strength of the research programme. This plurality of specialisms was augmented by the practical knowledge of the advisory committees associated with each project. These committees included teachers, researchers, lecturers, SEB officers and HMIs who offered the projects critical comment, concrete support and channels for dissemination of the findings. They were not, however, 'steering' committees and the research decisions remained the researchers' responsibility. This arrangement maintained the researchers' autonomy but ensured regular dialogue between them and practitioners about the projects' relevance to 'real-life' education.

Advisory committees apart, the research was scrutinized by many teachers, advisers and HMIs involved in curriculum developments and in-service. Furthermore, the appointment of a research adviser to the SED led to extra requests for research reports and opportunities for the adviser to observe the projects' field work. However wearisome such stringent accountability was to the researchers, it established contacts between them and the 'users'; these were particularly strong where teachers participated in collaborative action research projects.

Plans for wider dissemination of the projects' products and findings faced a choice between using commercial outlets or more informal channels. Many responded to understandable demands to make materials available rapidly and informally. Drawbacks to this strategy can arise from the costs and work involved in distribution, the unpolished appearance of some non-commercial publications, inadequate marketing or publicity machinery and the reluctance of publishers subsequently to adopt materials which had already been available to users in some cheap, preliminary form. Against this has be to balanced the delays and possible publishers' demands for changes in the materials normally associated with glossy, well-marketed publications.

A few projects were able to provide a basis for further funded research concerned with other ages (reading assessment techniques at primary level), wider application (computer assisted career guidance extended to England and Wales with the cooperation of the Department of Education and Science) or development in complementary areas (competence in spoken English leading to work on listening comprehension). In other cases, however, expertise has been lost where contract researchers have had to find other employment rather than build on and exploit their research findings. The follow-up to projects which explored the feasibility of resource provision was uneven. The establishment of item banks, for example, was dependent on commitments of local authorities to finance, and of colleges or universities to maintain and develop the resources. So far these commitments have not been made. Among the reasons for this have been: the reluctance of local authorities to commit themselves to financial backing until they saw the 'finished' article; the inexperience of researchers in 'selling' their products; doubts about the value of centralized item banks (teachers apparently prefer more modest resources within their control); and general shortage of funds. In contrast, the research on diagnostic assessment led to local authority support for a Schools' Assessment Research and Support Unit. Decisions to establish this lower cost, low technology unit with an in-service/developmental remit were easier.

It is clear that the main external pressures on the projects encouraged developmental work rather than research or evaluation. For example, although the action research projects were set up, in a context of school-based initiatives, to address such broad research questions as 'How can teachers be stimulated to undertake developments and adopt a reflective and critical stance towards their own teaching?', the researchers were urged to put most of their own efforts into development work. In particular, the scarcity of independent evaluation studies was a disappointment. Opportunities were missed to monitor JWP deliberations, teachers' curriculum/assessment decision making, new roles for school management, changes in teaching approaches, reactions of teachers to reversion from school-based to centralized curriculum planning and the evolution of whole-school assessment policies. A symptom of a felt need among the educational community for evaluation was manifest in the reactions to the research on collaboration in multi-disciplinary courses. This project was not conceived as an evaluation but its findings were taken up and treated as if they offered formative evaluation data.

The research programme's material support for the developments are evident. It is also plausible to argue that research played a central role in the changes in ideas which have been manifest in new HM Inspectorate policies for assessment which eschew norm-referencing, teachers' readiness to challenge the worth of single grade certificate awards, local authority financing of diagnostic assessment programmes and the discussions on the relevance of product-based external examinations for process-based curricula. The opportunities offered by the research to extend knowledge about curriculum and assessment have evoked compliments and envy from many outsiders. Murphy (1982), for example, after a major symposium on assessment and certification in the United Kingdom commented that when exposed to reports of the Scottish programme English eyes 'boggled and many reflected on the lack of co-ordinated post-Waddel 16+ examination research south of the border'.

It would be difficult to refute the claim that the research programme had a substantial impact on the thinking and practice of many teachers, lecturers, advisers and HMIs closely involved in the developments.

That impact was, no doubt, a contributing factor to the SED's new proposals for certification which attempted a compromise (through Grade-Related Criteria) between established, norm-referenced grades and criterion-referenced descriptions of performance. Nevertheless, the *direct* influence of research on major educational decisions is hard to assess. It is interesting that one project was commissioned to explore the feasibility of a fully criterion-referenced certificate and a commitment was made to use the project's interim report to inform decisions about the new certification. Those decisions, however, were taken before the date agreed for the production of the report.

From the researchers' point of view, this programme has illustrated something of the communication mechanism between policy-related research of this kind and central policy makers. The researchers have often felt remote from those who make the 'big' decisions and they have frequently perceived their work as having little direct impact on the thinking of senior members of HM Inspectorate, the SED administration or the SEB. To expect such direct impact on any significant scale in our existing system of education would be unrealistic. The 'big' decisions taken by senior people are primarily based on factors such as the policies of the party in government at the time, the views of various institutions in the system (e.g. teachers' unions, Scottish Universities Council on Entrance, HM Inspectorate, officials of SEB and the CCC) and their own experience of education. What this research programme has shown, however, is that research can have an *indirect* impact through the pressures exerted by various groups of practitioners. Even when research is firmly policy-related its findings have to be (and, in this case, have been) mediated through changes in practitioners' thinking. If this conclusion is valid then, given the system we have, researchers have to ensure that teachers, advisers, HMIs and development officers are informed, persuaded and mobilized by the research to bring their influence to bear on policy decisions. And that implies an exacting level of accountability for research as it is scrutinized by those at the chalk face.

From the perspective of those who set up policy-related programmes, I suggest that there are several lessons to be learned from this research enterprise. First, a pluralistic research element in a larger development programme can offer valuable support to teachers and others with responsibility for implementing the changes in curriculum and assessment; in this programme, this has been achieved by a relatively small number of people who clarify ideas, develop resources, explore teaching and assessment strategies, generate theory, stimulate action and investigate the implications of taking certain decisions. Secondly, there is a danger that pressures on research projects to concentrate on developmental activities will be at the expense of the long-term benefits of research and evaluation; failure to address research (as opposed to development) issues and to carry out independent evaluations of programmes will (i) do nothing to promote understanding of why things turned out the way they did, and (ii) severely limit what future developments can learn from earlier programmes. Thirdly, if government funded research as a whole is to be efficient and to build on the knowledge it generates through programmes of this kind, then it has to plan ahead to retain the researchers who have developed valuable expertise, and to promote new research projects or resource developments which explicitly make use of the programmes' findings. And finally, active and continuing dialogue about effective dissemination of research findings and material products has to be maintained; advisory committees with their wide representation of educators provide an excellent forum for discussion of the appropriate audience, timing, form and channels for dissemination for the products of projects.

Perhaps the lesson that all should learn from this programme of research is that it is very easy to expect too much of projects. In the first place, it is unrealistic to expect research to provide immediate solutions to the practical problems of teaching; its main strength must be in its potential to extend knowledge about education and so contribute to the basis on which decisions are made and classroom actions are planned in the longer term. In the second place, even in a programme of this size the human resources for research were limited. Many lecturers in universities and colleges have made considerable contributions, but their commitments to their projects could only be part-time and the main burden fell on full-time contract researchers. Even at the height of the programme's activities, the numbers of such researchers were little more than one per Scottish regional authority. There is no way that this small group could do more than offer a modest level of support, in the form of development materials and research findings, to the enormous population of secondary school teachers, administrators, examiners, government officers, and others who are faced with the prospect of making an alarming array of crucial decisions about the curriculum, assessment, certification and implementation of the innovations.

References

LEIGH, A. (1980). 'Policy research and reviewing services for under fives', *Social Policy and Administration,* 14, 162.
MURPHY, R. (1982). 'Assessment', *Research Intelligence,* 12, 6.

SCOTTISH EDUCATION DEPARTMENT (1977a). *The Structure of the Curriculum in the Third and Fourth Years of the Scottish Secondary School.* (The Munn Report). Edinburgh: HMSO.

SCOTTISH EDUCATION DEPARTMENT (1977b). *Assessment for All: Report of the Committee to Review Assessment in the Third and Fourth Years of Secondary Education in Scotland* (The Dunning Report). Edinburgh: HMSO.

SCOTTISH EDUCATION DEPARTMENT (1980). *The Munn and Dunning Reports: The Government's Development Programme.* Edinburgh: SED (mimeo).

SCOTTISH EDUCATION DEPARTMENT (1982). *The Munn and Dunning Reports: Framework for Decision.* Edinburgh: SED (mimeo).

CHAPTER 11
Innovation in the Balance

Sally Brown and Pamela Munn

Introduction

Our intention has been that the different chapters of this book should reflect several different perspectives on the recent developments in education for 14- to 16-year-olds in Scotland. As we stressed earlier, we are not claiming to offer a complete picture of the very ambitious programme, but we hope we have identified some of the dimensions of views held by people who have been involved in the events of the last few years in various capacities. The individual contributions reflect the views of their authors and, as editors, we do not necessarily agree with everything which has been said. We do believe, however, that all the arguments and opinions put forward are valuable expressions of alternative ways of looking at the programme and merit close attention.

In our introductory chapter, we made it clear that our interest was in a number of distinctive features of the developments and in the implications of these features for the professional lives of teachers; we have been concerned neither with documenting those aspects of the curriculum, assessment or teaching which remain unchanged nor with offering a comprehensive critique of the programme. In general, therefore, we wish to offer conclusions or summaries which are constructive and positive. The reason for introducing new developments, however, is invariably dissatisfaction with the status quo and most of the chapters are concerned with innovatory activities which arose, in part at least, from perceived weaknesses in previous educational practices. Before we offer a final summative commentary, therefore, we feel we should remind readers of the kinds of weaknesses in 14 to 16 educational provision identified by the authors.

Perceived Shortcomings of Previous Educational Practice

In some cases, the weaknesses were those of omission. Thus Pamela Munn and Douglas Weir have written about experiments in multi-disciplinary courses which came about because of recommendations of the value of such courses for a curriculum which had previously been characterized as 'single subject'. In a similar way, much of the other research in the programme arose because in the past certain kinds of learning and assessment had been neglected. Sally Brown's chapter has given an account of a whole series of projects which were concerned with conceptualizing pupil attainments which had not been previously clarified and with developing new types of assessment procedures.

Tom Johnson has pointed to a traditional gap in teachers' education. He has argued that while there had been rhetorical encouragement to teachers to facilitate pupils learning to discuss and learning through discussion, teachers did not have the necessary skills and understandings to implement such an approach. He has seen his involvement in in-service research, where teachers have developed awareness of discussion group processes and carried out school-based experiments, as a crucial experience. In the past, and without such experiences, he saw little alternative to teachers assuming that pupils must have derived communicative benefit from discussions even if this benefit could not be recognized; in practice, he believed, those discussions tended to reinforce the dominance or submissiveness of individual pupils.

Weaknesses in the sense of existing practices and ideas which should be changed, however, have been the more frequent objects of criticism that have weakness of omission. Eric Drever and Mary Simpson have both directed attention to the damage which they see done by the traditional assumption that some sort of 'general ability', intrinsic to the pupil and largely unchangeable, is the main determinant of pupils' performance. Both have argued that (i) diagnostic assessment of pupils' various specific capabilities and difficulties, and (ii) consideration of the nature and quality of the instruction which pupils receive, must be the first concerns in offering explanations of achievement or non-achievement. Mary Simpson has suggested that current strategies for teaching concept development are inadequate. She claims that this lack, together with unrealistic demands that pupils be taught concepts at an explanatory level, has led to over-simplification and fictionalization of those concepts. Both these authors have argued that most tests of attainment have been unsuitable for diagnostic assessment, and that the results of such tests will identify areas of failure without illuminating either the source of failure or the nature of appropriate remediation. Each of these contributions has looked at how assessment in existing circumstances can be improved so that it can be revitalized to have educational meaning. They also have considered ways in which a proper link can be forged between the primary function of assessment (to improve learning) and the nature and quality of the teaching.

Margaret Eleftheriou's contribution has demonstrated her awareness, as an English teacher, of the shortcomings of past assessment practices. In particular, she has criticized reading tests which on closer examination appear to test other things; poor performances on such tests in the past may well have been invalid indicators of poor readers. Her chapter has exemplified how the traditional emphasis on assessment as a summative activity at the end of a course and carried out by external experts is now under scrutiny from teachers. She has highlighted teachers' new concerns for identifying *what* is being tested by assessment and *who* is in the best position to take the responsibility for making valid assessments of different kinds of pupil attainments.

The contributions from Peter Martin and Donald McIntyre emerged from two broad areas of dissatisfaction with major aspects of the education sytem as a whole. These areas were identified in the Munn and Dunning Reports (and, indeed, to some extent by the much earlier *Report on Secondary Education* prepared by the Advisory Council on Education in Scotland in 1947). In the first place, there was concern that existing certification procedures exerted a profound influence on secondary education but (i) offered almost nothing in the way of descriptions of pupils' attainments, and (ii) for the most part paid attention to only those attainments which could be assessed by a relatively brief external examination. Peter Martin's chapter is concerned with the implications of replacing a traditional norm-referenced system of certification with a more descriptive criterion-referenced scheme, and with fostering valid internal assessment by teachers as a contribution to both certification and diagnosis of pupils' strengths and weaknesses. In the second place, Donald McIntyre has drawn attention to the lack of impact on educational practice which has characterized past policies for innovation that has not been school-based (whether in Scotland or elsewhere). His chapter is directed towards not just the idea of including the missing element of internal assessment for certification purposes, but also the broader possibilities for change arising from school-based development programmes.

These are the kinds of characteristics of existing practices in curriculum and assessment which stimulated the contributors to this book to be involved in the developments in the ways that they were. But what have their contributions to tell us about their perceptions of those five features of the programme which we described as 'distinctive' in Chapter 1? What, in the eyes of some of those involved in the programme, has emerged from (i) the experiments on more school-based procedures for development, (ii) the new emphasis on assessment as an integral part of the curriculum and support for learning, (iii) the call for certificates which provide descriptive accounts of pupils' attainments and assessments by teachers, (iv) the innovations in defining what counts as knowledge to be acquired by pupils, and (v) the inclusion in the main developments of a substantial programme of research to inform policy and practice?

An Experiment on School-Based Procedures for Development

Characteristics of School-Based Development Munn and Dunning Style

The dominant theme to emerge from the contributions as a whole is that of school-based development. For this reason we devote most space in our final chapter to this theme. School-based development had several different connotations in the context of the 'Munn-Dunning' programme, but the attempts to include a substantial number of teachers in extended dialogue and collaboration on development of curriculum, assessment and teaching approaches had three clear characteristics: first, the restriction of such activities to courses for the lowest achievers, i.e. Foundation level; secondly, the concentration of the dialogue and collaboration into the earliest stages of the developments; and thirdly, the limited range of subjects or courses in which school-based developments were tried.

The first of these is interesting because most of the pupils involved in such courses would have been described, on the old system, as 'less-academic' and, as Donald McIntyre points out, schools and teachers traditionally have had almost complete freedom to plan courses for such groups. The Dunning Report's recommendations attempted to remove the contrast between, on the one hand, the school-based courses and assessment for the 'less-academic' and, on the other hand, the centrally controlled syllabuses and certification for the 'academic' pupils. Thus the report suggested that the responsibility for syllabus planning and assessment for pupils at *all* levels of achievement be divided between schools and a central authority. Although the suggestion for collaboration with teachers was taken up in the feasibility studies at Foundation level, the distinction between different levels of achievement has been maintained by the government's rejection of the proposal for internal syllabuses and assessment at General or Credit levels (SED, 1980:7, with a minor modification to this for a small number of subjects at General level: see SED 1982:53).

The second characteristic, which places the school-based experiments early in the programme, is well documented in Margaret Eleftheriou's account of the feasibility studies in English. What is not clear is why the school-based procedures were so apparent then and not later on. Were there specific findings from the feasibility studies which led to the reversion to the more central development model? Were the constraints of time for development and implementation so acute that the only solution to the problem appeared to be direction from the centre? Or did the educational community at large misread the government's original intentions, and was the apparent move to investigate a more school-based model for development not that at all but rather a first 'pilot' stage in what was always planned to be a centralized programme?

The third characteristic of the school-based development experiments, the limited range of the subjects or courses involved, has been reflected in the subject-matter of this book. In particular, multi-disciplinary courses have been given attention out of proportion to their presence in the curriculum. Nevertheless, their 'newness' to the Scottish 14 to 16 curriculum (which Pamela Munn suggested had formerly interpreted 'multi-disciplinary' largely as collections of discrete subjects) made them an important facet of the development to explore and justified their 'headstart' in the programme. English, mathematics and science, in contrast with the multi-disciplinary courses, had powerful and academic traditions of courses, examinations and communities of specialist teachers. To put emphasis on these three is justified not only by the wide agreement that these are important 'core' subjects, but also by the interesting questions posed about the extent to which school-based developments should and could challenge the established content or approaches to teaching that have traditionally featured in these subjects. But what of the other courses not included in the feasibility studies? This book has nothing to say about school-based developments in these areas apart from some research initiatives in a very few schools. Other courses are now emerging from reports from central Joint Working Parties (JWPs) and Scottish Examination Board (SEB) panels. These reports are supplemented by some pilot work in schools carried out by HM Inspectorate. Such procedures illustrate rather nicely the classical centralized model of curriculum development.

In those circumstances where teachers and schools *were* actively involved in the decision making there emerged an encouraging scene. Margaret Eleftheriou's contribution offered a taste of the excitement, feeling of involvement and professional satisfaction which, despite the enormous amount of work demanded, the teachers took from their contributions to the feasibility studies. The early days seem to have been characterized by an unexpected openness and an eagerness on the part of HMIs to stimulate and use teachers' ideas. Pamela Munn also describes the satisfaction which Social and Vocational Skills (SVS) teachers felt in developing a course which was new, offering something of value to low achievers and, most importantly, *theirs*. It is interesting that SVS, which as Donald McIntyre has pointed out appears to be a truly school-based development, has captured the teachers' enthusiasm, sustained their sense of 'ownership' more than any other *and* was the one course for which the timetable for implementation was brought forward (by one year). This is in curious contrast to the widely held view that if one wants rapid innovation then one cannot leave it to the teachers: speed, it is believed, implies direction from the centre.

Whatever the limitations of the school-basedness of the programme as a whole there has been, as Donald McIntyre suggested, many more ideas shared among teachers and much thoughtful, enthusiastic and innovative teaching. Margaret Eleftheriou talked of reappraisals by teachers of English of their traditionally held values, and Pamela Munn has recounted how SVS teachers came to see themselves no longer as transmitters of knowledge but as providers of opportunities for pupils to construct their own knowledge from experiences. Even at the level of national certification, Peter Martin has remained convinced that teachers are in the best position not only to have a complete understanding of pupils' performance but also to make the crucial assessments for certification.

School-Based Development and Developments in Teaching Methods

But have school-based developments in teachers' thinking led to corresponding developments in classroom practice? The contributions to this book have provided some small-scale evidence of this kind, but only at the level of the individual teacher or school. On a national scale, we have little information to go on.

Tom Johnson has described how the developing awareness, among a group of teachers, of the processes of group discussions led to collaboration on practical schemes for improving pupils' awareness and skills in discussion in the classroom, and to a new classroom role for the teachers as a non-directive conductor of pupils' discussions. The teachers who had complete control of the developments in Eric Drever's work on mastery-learning, were able to suspend their belief in the power of 'general ability' to determine pupils' performance and to experiment creatively with the curriculum and assessment in classrooms. Their morale was increased by their own perceptions of the improvements in pupils' motivation and performance. One interesting feature of these two accounts is that although in both cases the teachers had in-service opportunities for reflection and thinking about their work, the customary in-service pattern of the intensive workshop was firmly rejected as unhelpful.

A second feature common to these two contributions, and to Pamela Munn's and Douglas Weir's accounts of SVS, was the evidence of a willingness among teachers to revise their notions about where the responsibility for decision making in the classroom lay. In the discussion groups there was an explicit initiative to ensure that pupils must not be dependent on the teacher, in the mastery-learning experiments teachers deliberately gave pupils responsibility for their own learning and in SVS were found the beginnings of a curriculum negotiated between teacher and pupil rather than imposed upon pupils.

Conditions for Effective School-Based Development

These kinds of accounts of instances of school-based developments are useful, but in the longer term it is an understanding of the conditions under which such developments are fostered or inhibited which is of most importance. The contributions to this book have offered information of three kinds which seem to be relevant to this issue on: local encouragements or constraints (e.g. time, timetables, resources, available teaching skills), teachers' own perceptions of the nature of their responsibilities as professionals and the influence of educational policies or other ad hoc decision making outside the school.

It is interesting how little attention has been drawn to problems of concrete material resources (although mountains of paper, typewriters and photocopies must have been essential). By far the most crucial concern of teachers was time. Margaret Eleftheriou has given a graphic account of the pressures on the teachers in the later stages of the feasibility studies as the pace of development was stepped up. The increase in the rate of distribution of documents and tasks from the centre drastically reduced the opportunities for teachers to examine them in detail, consider their implications or contribute creatively to the decisions which were being taken. In other circumstances, teachers were trying to formulate multi-disciplinary courses, generate strategies based on mastery-learning principles or develop diagnostic techniques, without, in their view, having enough time available to meet their deadlines. It is not that school-based innovation is more lengthy than centrally controlled innovation. The little evidence we have suggests it may be more efficient in effecting real change even in the short term. The problem here is that development deadlines which are fixed to conform to outside requirements are unlikely to match the pacing most appropriate for effective development in the schools. The effect has been to weaken the impact which teachers and schools have had on the decisions which have been made.

Teachers' commitments and contributions to the new and distinctive multi-disciplinary courses, as Pamela Munn points out, were also strongly influenced by the vagaries of school timetables. Opportunities for the necessary collaboration among teachers from different departments were greatly constrained if schools could not assign specific times for team meetings. Furthermore, the out of school experiences which pupils were intended to have in multi-disciplinary courses clearly required block timetabling of a sort that traditional single subject schemes are not set up to provide.

Even where local arrangements were made which were supportive of multi-disciplinary work, teachers were conscious of the need to supplement their existing skills and experience. Their growing awareness of the 'new' approaches identified for them gaps in their traditional training. The resources which appear to have offered some resolution to these problems are not those of a concrete material kind but rather innovative in-service initiatives such as those described by Tom Johnson and Douglas Weir. In each case, these have abandoned the structured workshops or talks from experts which have characterized Scottish in-service activity in the past; instead, the emphasis has been on providing conditions which encourage and facilitate teachers' reflection on and awareness of the processes of the 'new' approaches to teaching.

The role which teachers are able and willing to play depends, however, not only on the conditions under which they work and the support with which they are provided; their views of themselves as employees or professionals (to use Margaret Eleftheriou's phrase) are also crucial. The choice between the two may, of course, be influenced by other factors. For example, the evidence from the account of the feasibility study in English suggested that the increasing pace of the programme inevitably enhanced the 'employee' part of the role and inhibited the 'professional'. And Pamela Munn's chapter showed how the distinctive newness of SVS was correlated with teachers' readiness to take responsibility for the course; this contrasted with Contemporary Social Studies (CSS) and Health Studies (HS) where the qualities distinguishing them from the traditional curriculum were less obvious and the teachers looked for much more central direction.

School-Based Development in a Centralized Education System

It is not possible, of course, to offer clear predictions of how teachers' views of themselves as professionals or otherwise will influence their involvement in these or other developments in the future. What the contributions to this book can do, however, is to draw attention to the importance, for the planning of educational developments, of understanding and taking account of the ways in which teachers currently think about their responsibilities. As Pamela Munn pointed out, a role of 'partnership with the centre' was unfamiliar to Scottish secondary school teachers. They were accustomed to centrally controlled syllabuses for national certification and complete autonomy for non-certificate courses. In both cases, Donald McIntyre has argued, they had a generally accepted right to privacy in their classrooms. Teaching methods, therefore, were largely the teacher's own affair and 'knowledge' was something possessed by the specialist teacher who had a responsibility to pass it on to pupils. They would be reluctant, however, as Eric Drever has commented, to hold themselves accountable for pupils' achievements in learning.

This pattern has sustained very well the traditional system of Scottish secondary education. But that is not to say that this view of the teachers' role is inevitably enduring or pervasive. We have seen in this book examples of considerable changes in classroom practice and of teachers' readiness to develop and teach courses outside their specialist areas; this is particularly evident in cases where teachers have already had experience of the school-based Mode III of the Certificate of Secondary Education. From Margaret Eleftheriou and Tom Johnson, we have evidence of an extension of their classroom and development roles to include an in-service education function for other teachers. Nevertheless, it is necessary to consider, as Donald McIntyre has done, the conditions under which teachers can be expected to accept and make a contribution of substance to innovations initiated elsewhere.

Whatever the readiness or otherwise of teachers to collaborate actively in development, there clearly have been some decisions made by the executive branch of the government which have profoundly affected the course of events. For example, the decisions to carry out the experiments of the feasibility studies and to involve teachers in action research have resulted in a wave of participation by teachers as evidenced by almost all the contributions to this book. On the other hand, national decisions about certification and assessment have probably done little to encourage school-based initiatives. Margaret Eleftheriou gave a telling account of the dampening effect of the sudden appearance of Grade Related Criteria (GRC) and, given the decision to award single grade certificates based on GRC, Peter Martin expressed doubts about the chances of success for the Dunning Report's vision of the development of criterion-referenced assessment systems in schools. Even in SVS, where school-based development had its firmest hold, the introduction of a product-oriented external examination for a process-based course and the decision not to offer awards in SVS at the highest (Credit) certificate level have each exerted a curbing influence. Perhaps the most crucial factor, however, was identified by Donald McIntyre when he drew attention to the continuing practice which characterizes educational planning in Scotland and, in relation to all educational issues and problems, seeks a 'single national solution'. This quest for a single orthodoxy, whether concerned with curriculum assessment or certification, must inevitably inhibit real school-based developments which, by their nature, foster diversity.

All of the contributors to this book have seemed to agree with Donald McIntyre's statement that 'School-based development is, quite simply, the only kind of curriculum development which stands a chance of success.' His analysis of teachers' perceptions of the developments in some of the feasibility studies offered a constructive account of the conditions under which teachers saw the innovations as (i) not school-based, (ii) school-based but not under the teachers' control and burdensome, or (iii) school-based, under the teachers' control and satisfying. He has suggested, however, that subsequent central decisions have failed to take account of either this kind of information generated by the feasibility studies or all the teachers' constructive activity. If, as he has claimed, the important decisions about innovations have been firmly retained at the centre, then real developments in teaching and learning will be at risk. Given the evidence in this book, it is difficult not to conclude, as Mary Simpson has done, that real change is likely to result not from 'big bang' central curriculum development but rather local innovation in classrooms by practising teachers.

A New Conception of Assessment

To replace the notion of assessment as primarily 'testing' and as distinct from 'teaching' by a new conception which sees it as an integral part of the curriculum and a support for learning, is to inject a new optimism into education. It is to say that assessment should not be seen in simply functional terms (e.g. as a way of selecting pupils for tertiary education or providing reports to parents and employers); assessment should be planned and evaluated in terms of the meaning it conveys and its potential to improve learning. Assessment is of value because it offers a way of exploring why pupils have or have not succeeded in learning; if it is used so that teachers better understand the conditions under which their pupils learn, then they can better facilitate and support that learning. As Mary Simpson and Eric Drever have pointed out, better diagnostic assessment leads to less rather than more remedial teaching.

It is clear that many teachers are seeing assessment in a new light. Margaret Eleftheriou has told us how those involved in the feasibility study in English came to realize the flaws of traditional summative assessment. She described the welcome emphasis on formative or diagnostic assessment and the expansion of assessment into areas previously thought to be unassessable. In particular, she has documented the growing importance to be attached to 'internal' assessments carried out in schools. Pamela Munn and Tom Johnson have also charted teachers' evolving awareness that new ways of thinking about and carrying out assessment have to be devised for experiential or process-based learning, and that pupils' self-assessments may have an important part to play.

The 'optimistic' conception of assessment is most fully articulated in Bloom's mastery learning approaches. Eric Drever's account of an investigation of how the principles of mastery learning (as opposed to Bloom's specific procedures) could be implemented in Scottish classrooms, made it clear that several profound implications for assessment arise from assumptions that pupils' success on any given task is dependent on whether they have the specific prerequisites for that task rather than on their general innate ability. First, assessment is as likely to be carried out before as after instruction. Secondly, it must necessarily be criterion-referenced (i.e. describe what has been achieved) rather than norm-referenced (i.e. make comparisons among pupils). And thirdly, used diagnostically it has to be designed to explore why pupils have failed to learn. Mary Simpson's chapter has elaborated this last point: she has drawn attention to the importance of investigating why it is that 'wrong' answers should make sense to pupils, what they need to know to offer 'correct' answers and whether their learning experiences were sufficiently clear, unambiguous, salient and unconfused for them to be able to develop the necessary understandings.

All of this implies that diagnostic assessment has to be continuous, detailed and penetrating. The exacting demands which it makes on the teacher, however, are to be balanced by the advantages of much easier remediation once the source of the learning problem has been diagnosed, and of the enhanced learning afforded by a 'prevention rather than cure' strategy. This is all very well in theory, but in practice have teachers been willing and able to implement 'new' assessment as supports for learning? And have pupils recognized this supportive role or have they regarded it all as the same old tests, marks, grades and reports scene?

The experiments within the mastery-learning framework, described by Eric Drever, provided some encouraging results. The teachers involved in this work disregarded formal diagnostic tests and developed flexible, frequent and informal procedures. These procedures allowed them to develop a better understanding of the kinds of mistakes made by their pupils and, the teachers claimed, led to improved pupil performance. Diagnostic information was richer if pupils constructed their own answers (rather than checking alternatives in multiple-choice items) and, as they were given responsibility for some of their own assessments, pupils came to regard the enterprise as a help to their learning rather than as a grading exercise for the teacher's benefit. Furthermore, it is interesting that these apparent gains were not at the expense of the teachers. Not only were pupils reported to be more motivated, but the teachers also found some relief from 'the grind of retesting and reteaching disenchanted pupils'.

The work which has been reported by Mary Simpson and Eric Drever has had a number of helpful suggestions to make to teachers about diagnostic assessment. For example, giving pupils the task of carrying out some of the assessments of their own performance enables them to realize that diagnosis is a support to them and not a judgement upon them. From the teachers' perspective, it appears that listening to their pupils' talk is probably the most important single diagnostic activity.

As well as this constructive information, however, these two chapters have analysed some of the other factors which bear upon teachers' ability and willingness to implement diagnostic assessment and upon the likelihood of reaping the theoretical benefits of diagnosis. In the mastery-learning work teachers were reluctant to hold back, behind their age group, those pupils with learning difficulties no matter what the promises of improved performance. As well as this commitment to a strictly age-determined class organization, the constraints under which teachers work, Mary Simpson has suggested, make them examine their teaching in management rather than learning terms. Their concerns are with their own presentation of the proper information for pupils and with well-organized teaching. In consequence, they do not appreciate their pupils' inadequate concept development or acquisition of 'wrong' information, and they are not good at judging which topics pupils find easy or difficult. Eric Drever argued that some of the teachers' resistance to thinking about teaching from the mastery-learning/diagnostic assessment viewpoint derived from what was perceived as a threat that teachers would be held accountable for what their pupils had and had not learned. Even if a mastery-learning approach were followed, a perceived threat of this kind could incur changes in the teachers' educational goals to some 'lowest common denominator' which all pupils could be expected to achieve.

Throughout this section we have tended to emphasize the complementary nature of the work reported by Eric Drever and Mary Simpson. Both offered a picture in which diagnostic assessment had to be formulated to fulfil a specific purpose of identifying what the individual pupil knows in a particular context (rather than what he or she could remember of what they had been taught). Peter Martin's stance, however, was in some contrast to theirs. He accepted the importance of continuous and detailed assessment of pupils' progress to help learning, he agreed that for such assessment we must move away from traditional psychometric approaches but he argued that the pressures on teachers made it necessary that internal assessments in the school be used for the dual purposes of (i) internal elements for certification, and (ii) formative assessment. He has told us that realistically we cannot expect teachers to carry out both aspects of assessment unless they use a common set of procedures. The other two authors argued that diagnostic assessment calls for something different from anything that has so far been offered as suitable for certificate reports (which are designed to report what pupils have achieved in relation to what they have been taught).

We shall see. For the time being, we can certainly say that teachers are accountable in terms of providing internal assessments or estimates for certification for pupils and that will inevitably be their priority. Whether those assessments will be able to fulfil a diagnostic function, or whether there will be sufficient incentive to teachers to participate in an additional and more fundamental diagnosis of the causes of pupils' successes and failures, remains to be seen. In the meantime we shall turn our attention to the specific matter of certification.

Innovation in Certification

The new conception of assessment discussed in the previous section has been accompanied by new ideas about the nature of certification. An alternative model to that of our existing certificates has been the focus of Peter Martin's contribution. In its 'ideal' form such an alternative should be able to offer a comprehensive description, in all areas of the curriculum, of what every pupil has achieved in relation to what he or she has had the opportunity to achieve. It follows that (i) the certificate should mirror the curriculum to which that pupil has been exposed, and (ii) those with the responsibility for teaching the pupil will be in the best position to make valid assessments.

Proponents of such a model see major advantages arising from its adoption. First, certification would no longer 'label' pupils with a single grade; instead the reader of the certificate would have an account which could be interpreted in terms of what the pupil knew, could do or had experienced. Secondly, assessment for certification would draw closer to assessment for other purposes such as diagnostic assessment and curriculum evaluation. Thirdly, by according teachers the responsibility for major educational decisions such as certification their professionalism would be enhanced and this would result in the raising of standards in schools.

Sally Brown's description of the investment of resources into research on criterion-referenced certification and a range of other projects involving teachers in the development of assessment approaches and procedures has suggested that the SED took seriously this new model for certification. However, Peter Martin has demonstrated that the certificates which the government has decided to introduce are of a different kind. They will be based on Grade-Related Criteria (GRC) which he has described as being a hybrid. The final certificates for the new Standard Grade will allow some broad description of the pupil's performance, but the major prominence will be given to the single overall grade. Such a grade 'labels' the individual so that comparisons may be readily made among pupils on their overall performances. A further 'labelling' may arise from the particular areas of the curriculum in which the pupils receive their certificates. It has already been pointed out that the status of the multi-disciplinary courses and science will be sharply affected by the decision that they should be offered only at the two lower levels (Foundation and General). Conversely, physics, chemistry, biology and others offered only at the two higher levels (General and Credit) have their prestige enhanced. What is now proposed, therefore, is a compromise certificate which has made a gesture towards the provision of a description of the pupils' performance but which discriminates among pupils as much as, if not more than, the traditional certificate/non-certificate system.

Furthermore, the government has rejected the Dunning Report's recommendation that some responsibility be given to teachers for certification at all levels. Only at the lowest (Foundation) level has this been accepted. The retention of an external examination format at all levels may well distort the assessment in some areas of the new curricula. The demands of a *product-oriented* external assessment in Social and Vocational Skills, for example, were a cause of consternation among the teachers defending their *process-oriented* course.

There were, of course, many entrenched practices and competing demands on certification which could be seen as inhibiting the emergence of a more radical system of certification. One major advantage of traditional certification has been the administrative convenience of dealing with single grades. Peter Martin has made it clear that while the major strength of a criterion-referenced system would be the provision of meaningful information about pupils' attainments, the foremost problem it faces is how to present all the detail it contains in a manageable form. Grade Related Criteria (GRC) are superficially attractive because they apparently offer the concise single grade *and* a description of performance. They rest, however, on the very dubious assumptions that (i) attainments in all elements of all courses can each be conceptualized at six different levels, and (ii) attainments in different elements of the same course can be aggregated to provide an overall grade which has educational meaning. There is a danger which could arise when GRC turn out not to be the expected panacea: we could regress into the worst of traditional norm-referencing for certification which, at best, would divorce assessment for certification from assessment for other purposes, or, at worst, would ensure that assessment for certification is the only assessment to receive attention.

We have already discussed the ways in which the initial moves to foster school-based developments have seemed to have been retracted. Similarly there is still a reluctance to trust teachers with the responsibility for certification except at the lowest levels of pupil achievement. Peter Martin is hopeful that the government will change its position on this point but he argues that it will be necessary to allow schools some flexibility in defining their own main skills (or 'aspects') and criteria for assessment. This flexibility is a necessary feature of giving teachers real professional responsibility for certification and, it is argued, of providing the conditions for raising standards in schools. But such flexibility inevitably leads to diversity among schools and makes comparisons across schools difficult. For the time being, it appears that our certification system will continue to put more emphasis on maintaining uniformity across schools through external assessments than on the provision of full descriptions of pupils' achievements and the improvement of teachers' professionalism through teachers' criterion-referenced assessments of performance.

One rather interesting feature of the references to certification in this book is the continuing use of the terms 'Foundation', 'General' and 'Credit'. The published arrangements for certification at Standard Grade are presented in terms of grade levels (1 to 6) and mention of Foundation, General and Credit awards is muted. Nevertheless, the three terms seem to have become part of the woodwork of Scottish education, and the contributors to this book are not alone in retaining them as characteristics of the new conception of education 14 to 16.

The Innovations in Defining What Counts as Knowledge

We indicated in our introductory chapter that the Munn Committee identified four main sets of aims for secondary schools in constructing a curriculum for 14- to 16-year-olds. These were (i) the development of knowledge and understanding, both of the self and the physical environment; (ii) the development of skills, cognitive, interpersonal and psychomotor; (iii) the affective development of pupils; and (iv) the equipping of young people with knowledge and skills which enables them to perform the various roles which life in their society entails. The committee stressed that all four sets of aims were equally important in constructing a curriculum and explicitly warned against elevating any one set to the status of an educational *summum bonum* ignoring, or undervaluing, others. Indeed, the committee deplored 'the pursuit of knowledge [being] conducted in a way which cultivates no skill other than the ability to memorise and recall and which develops no affective quality, apart, possibly, from the capacity to tolerate boredom, and which divorces knowledge so totally from the social realities of the pupils' experience that its contribution to the development of social competence is minimal; if it exists at all' (SED, 1977, para.4.8). What can be gleaned from the various contributions to this book about new conceptions of knowledge in the development programme? In particular, is there evidence of definitions of knowledge which move away from the emphasis on the ability to memorize and recall?

First, it is clear from Margaret Eleftheriou's account of developments in English, that the programme provided opportunities for reconceptualizing English as a subject. This is evident in the central importance attached to defining the subject in terms of the four modes, reading, writing, listening and talking. These modes provided both the framework for a critical analysis of previous work in English at Bankhead and the means for 'allowing the poor reader/learner into a previously inaccessible world'. All four modes were regarded as equally important and the fact that listening stood out as 'virtually unknown and untried' encouraged experiments in teaching and assessing listening skills. Bankhead's involvement in 'Munn and Dunning' then, undoubtedly promoted and encouraged new and wider definitions of what was to count as English. It also encouraged a fundamental reconsideration of how to assess pupils' abilities in English given this wider definition of the subject.

Secondly, the programme signalled its desire to explore new definitions of knowledge by including multi-disciplinary courses in the early curriculum developments. Two of these courses, Health Studies and Social and Vocational Skills (SVS) directed attention to knowledge in areas traditionally neglected in Scottish secondary schools. Given the concern about Scotland's appalling health statistics and the emphasis on the relevance of the school curriculum, both these courses could be interpreted as a direct response to the kinds of omissions in the curriculum mentioned in the Munn Report (SED, 1977). The third course, Contemporary Social Studies, could be seen as a direct response to the report's call for 'units of work which deal with the political, economic, industrial and environmental aspects of life in modern society' (SED 1977, para.5.18). It is fair to say, however, that for many social subjects teachers, this title did not in itself represent a new definition of knowledge. Not only did modern studies (a course already available to 14- to 16-year-olds) explicitly deal with contemporary society, but many non-certificate courses in the social subjects focused on this area. The multi-disciplinary courses, however, provided opportunities for new definitions of knowledge which extended beyond their titles.

SVS, perhaps the most radical of the three courses in this context, saw knowledge as something acquired individually by pupils through reflection upon various experiences they had engaged in as a consequence of participation in the course. Knowledge was not seen as a commodity to be transmitted by the expert teacher to the lay pupil, whose task it then was to reproduce it more or less accurately. There were no 'right answers' to written or spoken reflections on visits to old people's homes, centres for the mentally handicapped or work experience. Even in situations where there were 'right answers' in the sense of the best tool to use for a particular job, for instance, these answers were to be taught and learned in 'real life' situations, such as home decorating, where improvisation and experiment were seen as part of real life.

In Health Studies and Contemporary Social Studies, their very multi-disciplinary nature offered teachers opportunities for examining and implementing new definitions of knowledge. The coordination and sometimes even the integration of the disciplines contributing to these courses meant that an alternative to a subject specific approach to knowledge could exist, at least in theory. Some teachers believed that by collaborating on syllabus construction for the courses something more than an amalgam of the subject contributions was achieved. At a lower level, topics such as diet or physical fitness could be admirable vehicles for welding the inputs of biology, home economics and physical education into a coherent whole and for applying the contributions of these subjects to 'the social realities of pupils' experiences' as the Munn Committee had suggested. Similarly, the study of a contemporary issue such as Northern Ireland could provide the focus for an amalgam of history, geography and modern studies in a way that helped pupils to make sense of media coverage of the issue. All three multi-disciplinary courses then, by their focus on areas such as health and social interaction, and by their involvement of a number of separate disciplines, provided opportunities for experimenting with new approaches to knowledge and relating that knowledge to pupils' lives.

A third way in which the government's programme encouraged new definitions of knowledge was through supporting innovative teaching approaches such as the learning to discuss and learning through discussion projects described by Tom Johnson. Here, learning to discuss was seen not only as a worthwhile skill in its own right, but also as an important means of promoting learning in other subjects. Like SVS, the discussion skills projects have focused on process more than on substantive content, paying more attention to *how* pupils learn and deliberately playing down the traditional emphasis on *what* pupils learn where this is conceived as pre-specified chunks of information to be transmitted to pupils. In these projects substantive content is a vehicle for opening up processes of self analysis and reflection, whether they be discussion skills, social interaction or work experience, not an end in itself. Indeed, these projects report the benefits to be gained from drawing pupils' attention to processes. Tom Johnson describes how pupils came to realize that their knowledge and performance could be improved as they became aware of group processes: dominant group members became aware that they had to learn to listen, the more silent pupils realized that they could make valuable contributions. The new definitions of knowledge then, included a new emphasis that knowledge can arise from pupils' own efforts to reconstruct their experience, and does not necessarily have to be poured into pupils by the knowledgeable teacher.

Lastly, the various assessment initiatives in the government's development programme, which have been described, have helped to keep definitions of knowledge high on the agenda. Work on diagnostic assessment has focused attention on the process of learning with Mary Simpson viewing pupils as 'continuous creators of their own understanding, rather than passive, imperfect accumulators of given knowledge'. This phrase, which so neatly sums up the tenets of SVS and discussion skills projects, illustrates the way in which assessment can support and even inform innovative definitions of knowledge. Similarly the conern with criterion-referencing and Grade-Related Criteria provides opportunities for defining the aims and intentions' of teaching the various subjects more precisely and thus for reconceptualizing them.

The danger is, of course, that aspects of courses which are not to be assessed, are down graded or disregarded. Such aspects can come to be seen as unimportant because they are not to be assessed. Thus the very essence of courses such as SVS or discussion risks being lost because self analysis and reflection are not being assessed, while skills in map reading or wiring a plug are. We are not trying to argue here that attempts should necessarily be made to assess new kinds of knowledge. Rather we are speculating that these new kinds of knowledge or process risk being undervalued in an age when a dominant concern is with assessment and certification. Teachers involved in developing and implementing these innovative definitions of knowledge are only too well aware of this danger, but there are other dangers too facing those who want to maintain new definitions of knowledge in the school curriculum.

Perhaps the most obvious danger is the unavailability of certification at the highest level for some of the courses trying to exemplify new definitions of knowledge. Multi-disciplinary courses like others adopting a generalist approach, such as courses in science for instance, are to be certificated only at Foundation and General levels while single subjects contributing to these courses will be certificated at Foundation, General and Credit. This must be interpreted as an implicit message that really worthwhile knowledge is subject specific and that academic excellence is associated with specialization. The danger is, then, that through its present certification policy, the government will choke off the very innovations in defining what counts as knowledge it has promoted.

There is a growing literature too, that suggests that new forms of knowledge in the social and life skills area can all too easily degenerate into attempts to instil social conformity in pupils in a way that suggests a marked shift in the rhetoric if not in the reality of the liberal traditions of education in this country. (See for example Bates *et al.,* 1984 and Watts, 1984.) The same literature also suggests, however, that new approaches to defining knowledge, which involve application of knowledge to real-life situations and which pose real problems to be solved, have been greeted enthusiastically by pupils with different kinds of abilities.

Other problems concerning the implementation and maintenance of new definitions of knowledge have emerged from the various contributions to this book. These problems range from those of school organization and management, providing time for multi-disciplinary course planning and teaching, for instance, to teachers' subject specific training, and to teachers' belief in the notion of pupils' general ability as a powerful explanation of their failure to learn.

It would be a pity if the enthusiasm and commitment of new definitions of knowledge displayed by those actively involved in pioneering new courses and/or teaching approaches were to be lost in the multiple developments in single subjects now taking place. It is clear from previous chapters that new definitions of knowledge have much to offer both to teachers and pupils. Their survival as new definitions is not unproblematic, however.

The Research Programme

It is significant that almost all the contributions to this book have referred directly to the research programme set up to support and inform 'Munn and Dunning' activities. That research played a part in helping teachers not only to implement and sustain various aspects of the government's programme but also to reflect on their own activities within the programme is clear. Accounts of collaborative action research by Eric Drever and Douglas Weir probably convey this most explicitly, but it is apparent that both Tom Johnson and Margaret Eleftheriou, for instance, have been engaged in research in their own classrooms. At the level of raising teachers' consciousness about their own practice and helping them to reflect on various aspects of their practice, the research programme may well have acted as a catalyst in the context of the various 'Munn and Dunning' developments.

At another level too, the research programme has provided immediate practical support for teachers in the shape of materials for say, the item banks in science and mathematics. It has also provided support for teachers of age groups outwith, as well as within the 14 to 16 band through fundamental work on conceptualising and assessing reading, for instance. At the classroom level then, it seems plausible to suggest that some of the research programme has had an impact on the reality of 'Munn and Dunning' both in terms of curriculum and assessment.

Chapter 10 makes it clear that it is extremely difficult to assess the impact of the research programme on policy making at a national level. It also identifies the tensions between those concerned with development, with getting things going, and those concerned with finding out what is taking place and why things turn out the way they do. In our view, research is better suited to increasing our understanding of such matters as teachers' classroom processes, or practical problems; far less is it able to provide a blueprint for successful innovation. The main strength of research lies in its potential to extend our understanding of teaching and learning and thus help to inform policy and practice so that we can in some sense improve our schooling. It is in this context that the paucity of evaluation studies is most to be regretted. The opportunity to study major innovations such as Joint Working Party deliberations, new roles for school management, teachers' classroom decision making and all the rest outlined has been lost. Our understanding of major features of schooling in the context of a national programme of innovation has consequently been impoverished, and we have missed the opportunity to learn as much from our current experience as we might have done.

All in all then, we would contend that the research programme has provided support in a variety of ways for teachers implementing Munn and Dunning; it has highlighted some tensions between those whose primary concern is pressing on with the development programme and those who seek to understand why things turn out the way they do; it has been available to inform policy although it is difficult to assess the extent to which it has done so; finally, impressive and extensive as the programme is, it would have exhibited these characteristics even more if it had included more evaluation studies.

In Conclusion

It would be difficult not to conclude that Scottish education has come a long way since the debut of the Munn and Dunning double act in 1977 and, as we have said elsewhere, nothing will ever be quite the same again. The extent to which educational practitioners have responded to a call to scrutinize, develop and give accounts of the curricula and assessments which are offered in our schools has been unprecedented. But we have by no means reached the new Jerusalem and considerable regrets have been expressed in this book and elsewhere about what might have been if only . . .

What can be said is that we have never before attempted a programme of national reform on this scale, and its strength has been the profound impact it has had on the thinking of a very large proportion of the educators in this country. Its success will not be constrained by the quality of the educational ideas which are now permeating the system. But that success will only be assured if administrators and politicians display insight and good judgement by giving precedence to educational goals before bureaucratic or political expediency.

References

BATES, I., CLARKE, J., COHEN, P., FINN, D., MOORE, R. and WILLIS, P. (1984). *Schooling for the Dole? The New Vocationalism.* Basingstoke: Macmillan.

SCOTTISH EDUCATION DEPARTMENT (1977). *The Structure of the Curriculum in the Third and Fourth Years of the Secondary School* (The Munn Report). Edinburgh: HMSO.

SCOTTISH EDUCATION DEPARTMENT (1980). *The Munn and Dunning Reports: The Government's Development Programme.* Edinburgh: SED (mimeo).

SCOTTISH EDUCATION DEPARTMENT (1982). *The Munn and Dunning Reports: Framework for Decision.* Edinburgh: SED (mimeo).

WATTS, A.G. (1984). *Education, Unemployment and the Future of Work.* Milton Keynes: Open University Press.

Biographical Notes on the Contributors and Editors

Editors

Sally Brown is a senior research fellow in the education department of the University of Stirling. Over the last 15 years she has been involved in a number of major research projects including an investigation of criterion-referenced assessment. She has published a wide range of articles and monographs in the broad areas of assessment, curriculum innovation and science education. Latterly she has been seconded to the Scottish Education Department as research adviser and has had responsibility for setting up and managing the Munn/Dunning research programme. She is currently involved in research on teachers' professional craft knowledge.

Pamela Munn is a lecturer in applied research in education at the University of York. Her research career in education began at the University of Stirling where she was a research fellow on a project on accountability funded by the then SSRC. This work was preceded by six years of history teaching in two London comprehensive schools where she latterly combined history teaching with a head of sixth form post. Her most recent research, on multi-disciplinary courses, was funded by the Scottish Education Department as part of the Munn/Dunning research programme.

Other Contributors

Eric Drever is lecturer in education at the University of Stirling. After graduating from Glasgow University he taught chemistry and general science in Glasgow schools from 1962 to 1972, and also worked as an examiner for the Scottish Examination Board. His main interests both in teaching and research are science teaching, teacher education, and assessment and evaluation, with an emphasis on the secondary sector.

Margaret Eleftheriou took a somewhat circuitous route (three years in the Foreign Office, residence in France and a M.A. (Hons) in French) to reach her first teaching post as an assistant teacher of English at Aberdeen

Academy in 1963. A four-year spell as assistant head of the English department at Harlaw Academy, Aberdeen, under the direction of Andrew Bruce, head of department, led to the experimental introduction of mixed ability groupings in third year classes and to the testing of the new proposals in Higher English (both of which led to quite unexpected conclusions). Since 1979 she has been head of the English department at Bankhead Academy, Aberdeen, where she has been responsible for the introduction and development of an integrated humanities course in S1 and S2.

Tom Johnson has been head of the department of modern studies at James Gillespie's High School in Edinburgh since 1977. He was assistant head of department from 1975, and before this his first teaching post was in Edinburgh's last junior secondary, David Kilpatrick, in 1972. Tom has served on a number of committees at a regional and national level and presently he is chairman of the Lothian branch of the Modern Studies Association. His long standing interest in extending the scope of modern studies is reflected in his commitment to including verbal communication skills in its curriculum. He believes that many types of verbal communication may be identified, that teacher training programmes can be developed in this area, and that verbal communication programmes should be an integral part of any social curriculum.

Donald McIntyre is reader in the education department of the University of Stirling. His extensive research experience includes investigations of the implementation across the secondary school curriculum of mastery learning and criterion-referencing approaches to teaching and learning and of other attempted innovations in secondary school science and modern languages teaching. His long standing interest in Munn and Dunning developments is reflected in his editorship of a critique of the reports in 1978.

Peter Martin is a lecturer is psychology at Jordanhill College of Education, one of Scotland's major teacher education colleges. His substantial research experience includes work on the psychology of music although he is best known for his work on assessment. This work includes a spell at the Scottish Council for Research in Education where he was involved in the Pakistan Primary Education Project. He spent some time in Pakistan researching assessment in primary schools. He is currently a co-director of two research projects on assessment funded by the Scottish Education Department, namely criterion-referenced assessment in geography and criterion-referenced certification.

Mary Simpson left school at 16 years of age to work in a microbiology laboratory. She gained H.N.C. (Chemistry) by day release and subsequently was awarded the degrees of M.A. (Hons.) and Ph.D. in psychology from Aberdeen University. Her research interests then, and since, have been with the mechanisms of perception, recognition, memory and learning. She became involved in educational research in 1976 when, with funding from the Scottish Education Department, she joined the staff of the biology department of Aberdeen College of Education in investigations of pupil learning difficulties and their diagnosis.

Douglas Weir and Bob Currie work in the Vocational Initiatives Unit at the University of Glasgow. Douglas Weir has long experience in educational research with a continuous commitment to identifying ways in which the curriculum for 14- to 18-year-olds can be made more relevant to them, while Bob Currie has long experience as a secondary school teacher, supplemented by considerable practical experience in curriculum development. Until recently they worked together in the Scottish Vocational Preparation Unit of which Douglas was Director. Currently they are collaborating to support the efforts of a large number of the Scottish local authorities which have undertaken projects within the Technical and Vocational Education Initiative (TVEI).

Index